GREEN & GOLDEN

PORTLAND TIMBERS' HISTORIC MARCH TO THE MLS CUP

OREGONLIVE

The Oregonian

ON THE COVER (ABOVE): Timbers players celebrate after winning the MLS Cup final 2-1 against the Columbus Crew at MAPFRE Stadium in Columbus, Ohio, on Dec. 6.

Thomas Boyd/The Oregonian/OregonLive

LEFT: Timbers defender Liam Ridgewell kisses the MLS Cup in celebration of the team's victory.

Randy L. Rasmussen/The Oregonian/OregonLive

Published by Pediment Publishing, a division of The Pediment Group, Inc. www.pediment.com. Printed in the United States.

Foreword

I was there five years ago when Timbers owner Merritt Paulson went on the road to Colorado for the very first game for his Major League Soccer franchise. You could tell he already loved the thing. Maybe it was all the legwork Paulson had to do in order to bring MLS to Portland. Maybe it was because the young owner sensed that this was finally his opportunity to do something that mattered.

Paulson was ready.

Portland fans were ready, too.

But the Timbers were not.

The record will show that the first goal in Portland's MLS history came in the 80th minute that first night off a free kick from Kenny Cooper. This was preceded by a 79-minute coma. But it's my memory of Paulson as he arrived well dressed and hopped-up on nervous energy that evening that I thought about five years later as he won his first championship.

The Timbers drew the Rapids — the defending MLS champions — in that MLS opener. Colorado decided to use the event to not only christen the Timbers with a 3-1 beatdown but also to hold a lengthy ceremony in which the Rapids unveiled their MLS Cup banner in front of the league's expansion entry. If that weren't enough, when Paulson went looking for the visiting owner's box before kickoff he was told that there wasn't one. And so the first revealing moment of Timbers MLS history began with the team owner muttering while lugging a folding chair along the third deck of the stadium. Paulson set up on press row, not far from my seat, where he and his staff sat and took in the game.

Today, Paulson's franchise is MLS champion. The legend might go that in just five short years Paulson went from sitting on a folding chair to lounging in the owner's suite at the MLS Cup title game watching Diego Valeri score a remarkable goal just 27 seconds in. Except, history often isn't that tidy and clean. Of course, Valeri scored. Of course, it was stunning. Of course, Paulson had an owner's box for the 2015 MLS Cup, he just wasn't sitting in it as kickoff started in Columbus.

Instead, this time Paulson found himself on the field taking part in the traditional ceremony before the league's final match, then scrambling to get to his seat.

"It was really congested getting off the field," Paulson told me later. "I finally said, 'Screw this, I'm not missing one minute of this.' I climbed over the railing in front of security guards and went up running though fans, which was probably not the most owner-like, civilized thing to do. But I was at a dead sprint into my box two seconds into kickoff, went running down to my seat and looked down and watched as Valeri scored and I was like, 'You gotta be kidding me' and by the time I was done celebrating that I was watching Rodney Wallace put a header in."

Turns out, this time Paulson wasn't ready.

But his MLS franchise finally was.

John Canzano
The Oregonian/OregonLive

Table of Contents

PLAYER PROFILES

ABOVE: Fanendo Adi heads the ball against the LA Galaxy on March 15 at Providence Park. Adi scored both goals for the Timbers in the 2-2 tie. Thomas Boyd/The Oregonian/OregonLive

OPPOSITE: Fanendo Adi grabs Timber Joey's chainsaw after scoring two consecutive goals as the Timbers beat the Seattle Sounders, 4-1, at Providence Park on June 28. Randy L. Rasmussen/The Oregonian/OregonLive

Fanendo Adi: From remote Nigeria to center stage, Timbers forward stands tall

By Jamie Goldberg

Portland Timbers forward Fanendo Adi lifted his arms in elation and ran toward the sideline smiling from ear to ear. His teammates followed, embracing him in a giant hug as they jumped up and down in excitement.

The 25-year-old had just scored the go-ahead goal off a penalty kick to give the Timbers a 2-1 lead over the reigning MLS Cup Champion LA Galaxy in Los Angeles. This, a scant three minutes after Adi had recorded the equalizer, turning and firing a beautiful left-footed shot into the net.

On the field, he exuded confidence.

"Adi has never been more bought in," Timbers coach Caleb Porter said. "He loves it here. He wants to win. Guys love him. He's playing hard. He's playing big."

Before the Timbers went on their incredible late-season run, Adi had been the main offensive weapon in an otherwise lackluster Timbers attack. He finished the regular season with a team-leading 16 goals. It was his offensive attack that helped lead the Timbers back above the red line in the Western Conference standings.

And Adi couldn't be happier.

After spending six years bouncing around different clubs in Europe looking for the right fit, Adi feels like he belongs in Portland.

"All along, I've been trying to find a perfect fit and I think here is a great fit for me," Adi said. "I'm pleased to be in Portland."

• • •

Adi grew up playing soccer, barefoot, in a remote village in Benue State, which sits in the middle of Nigeria.

When his parents sent him on errands, the budding soccer star would often get sidetracked and instead end up playing soccer in the streets. He would spend hours running up and down the sandy lots alongside other children, completely forgetting about the errands, even though he knew he'd be in trouble when he came home.

Adi still remembers his first pair of "cleats." The shoes were a gift from a friend and Adi was so excited to have real boots that he didn't even realize that they were American football cleats. The first time he went in for a tackle, he accidentally cut his opponent's leg with

ABOVE: Fanendo Adi celebrates after scoring late in the second half against the New England Revolution on June 6 at Providence Park. Adi scored both of Portland's goals in the last four minutes of regulation time, and the Timbers won 2-0.
Thomas Boyd/The Oregonian/OregonLive

OPPOSITE: Fanendo Adi celebrates his go-ahead goal in the 90th minute against the LA Galaxy on March 15 at Providence Park. LA tied the score in stoppage time two minutes later for a 2-2 final score.
Thomas Boyd/The Oregonian/OregonLive

the spikes.

"They looked like soccer shoes,'" Adi said. "I was excited because basically before that I played without shoes."

Despite his humble beginnings, Adi quickly rose up the ranks. An agent noticed him playing when he was 15 and invited him to tryout in Lagos, Nigeria's teeming metropolis.

Adi's parents weren't pleased. They wanted their son to focus on his education and earn a college degree. But Adi couldn't pass up the chance to chase his dream.

"My family didn't want me to travel anywhere to go play football," Adi said. "They wanted me to go to school. At the end of the day, I had to lie to my family to go play football."

Adi arrived at the tryout expecting to be one of 65 players competing for 10 spots in the Brazilian Soccer School, a well-regarded soccer academy in Lagos. Instead, 400 boys showed up.

The lean and tall striker had just 10 minutes to show off his skills, but it was enough.

"Out of 400 players, he ended up choosing just me," Adi said. "I was the one that came from a very small village and became the chosen one out of 400."

Adi spent the next six months honing his game at the Brazilian Soccer School, before being sent to a tryout for second-division club AS Trenčín in Slovakia. The tryout lasted just 30 minutes, but once again Adi made an impression.

He was offered the chance to leave Nigeria to play professional soccer.

• • •

In 2014, Adi was offered the chance to join Danish Superliga side FC Copenhagen. He traveled to Den-

FANENDO ADI

Age: 25
Height: 6'4"
Position: Forward
Birthplace: Benue State, Nigeria
Fanendo Adi Trivia: He set a Timbers MLS club record with 16 goals in 2015.

2015 Stats
Regular-Season Goals: 16
Regular-Season Assists: 3
Postseason Goals: 2
Postseason Assists: 1

mark excited to continue to build his career in Europe, but the coach who brought Adi to Copenhagen was fired only days after he arrived.

A new coach came in with his own crop of players and style of play and Adi realized that he might need to look for another opportunity.

When he was offered the chance to come to the United States and join the Timbers, he jumped at it.

"Coming to America was a decision that was very easy, knowing that the club wanted me and the coach wanted me," Adi said.

In his first games in Portland, Adi made enough of an impression to earn a contract.

But Adi's transition to MLS wasn't seamless. The striker went through long scoreless droughts in 2014 and early 2015.

Still, over time, Adi has shown just how valuable he can be for the Timbers.

Adi is still young and Porter said he is continuing to evolve. This year, Porter tried to help Adi simplify his game and worked on finding ways to play to his strengths. He would send Adi a text before every game, reminding the 6-foot-4 striker to "play big."

"He's a guy that as big as he is, sometimes he doesn't play that big or in the past he hasn't," Porter said. "But he's learning to embrace how big and strong and mean he can be."

Adi has never felt more motivated to succeed.

He has grown into his shoes and is living out his dream.

"In soccer, nothing is easy," Adi said. "Of course, we've had our ups and downs, but I came here to play and that's just what I'm doing." ∎

ABOVE: Fanendo Adi battles Seb Hines of Orlando City SC on April 12 at Providence Park. Thomas Boyd/The Oregonian/OregonLive

ABOVE LEFT: Fanendo Adi gets set to boot the ball against Real Salt Lake at Providence Park on March 7. Thomas Boyd/The Oregonian/OregonLive

OPPOSITE: Fanendo Adi controls a pass against Victor Bernardez of the San Jose Earthquakes. Adi received the team's "Golden Boot" award for 2015 as the club's leading scorer, setting a new mark for most goals in a regular season with 16. Randy L. Rasmussen/The Oregonian/OregonLive

Nat Borchers: Timbers' biggest offseason addition feels at home in Portland

By Jamie Goldberg

As spring turned to summer in 2014, Nat Borchers and his wife, Crystal, began to notice the ominous signs on the horizon.

Over the previous seven years, Borchers had grown to call Salt Lake City home. Crystal had left a steady job in Colorado to join Borchers in Utah and the couple had married, bought a house and developed a network of friends. Their first child was due later that summer and the couple had every intention of raising him in the congenial city of Salt Lake.

But Borchers' contract with Real Salt Lake was set to expire at the end of the year and the club hadn't given the veteran defender any indication they were planning to re-sign him.

"We just built up so many good relationships and we thought for sure we were going to be there the rest of our lives," Borchers said. "To realize that, 'Wow, we're maybe not as wanted as we thought we were,' it was definitely tough."

At the end of 2014, Real Salt Lake offered Borchers a stark choice. Instead of leaving the fan favorite unprotected in the expansion draft, the club could trade him, and Borchers could have a say in picking his new city.

Throughout his long career, Borchers had engaged in a constant battle to prove himself. Now, the 33-year-

old would have to start over. But he saw the change as an opportunity to join a club brimming with immense potential.

With the Portland Timbers, he believed he could be part of something special.

• • •

In November 2006, Crystal Chavez was chatting with her sister at a bar in Pueblo, Colorado, when she noticed a familiar face across the room.

She had been a grade above Borchers in high school and the two weren't friends, but she still recognized him immediately. After a lot of coaxing from her sister, Crystal decided to walk over and say hi.

After going undrafted in the 2003 MLS SuperDraft, Borchers had earned a tryout with the Colorado Rapids and fought to not only earn a roster spot, but become a

starter. After three years with the Rapids, he had signed with Norwegian Tippeligaen club Odd Grenland, hoping the move could serve as a stepping stone.

Borchers had returned to his hometown of Pueblo

ABOVE: Timbers defender Nat Borchers started to think of Portland as home after scoring a goal in an Aug. 15 game against his former team, Real Salt Lake. Beth Nakamura/The Oregonian/OregonLive

OPPOSITE: Nat Borchers celebrates his first goal of the season against FC Dallas on April 4 at Providence Park. It was also the first of three goals the Timbers would score in their 3-1 win for their first victory of the 2015 season. Thomas Boyd/The Oregonian/OregonLive

KING OF BEARDS

after his first season in Norway and was feeling pretty smug. He figured by now, everyone in his hometown must know he had made it as a pro soccer player.

In the loud bar, Crystal asked him what he'd been up to and he told her he was visiting from Norway, assuming she knew about his soccer career. Crystal heard "Ordway," not Norway, a town in Colorado notorious for its prison.

"I went back to my sister and said, 'I guess he might be a prison guard,'" Crystal said. "I still went on a first date with him."

Soon after they started dating, Borchers returned to Norway for a second season. Though he felt his soccer had improved, Borchers had struggled adapting to the foreign culture and language and felt isolated in the small city of Skien.

He called Crystal from his apartment and dejectedly told her he wanted to quit soccer.

"I was literally to the point where I was just so frustrated with the situation," Borchers said. "Real Salt Lake called at the exact right time."

• • •

Salt Lake had been a perennial bottom-dweller during its first three seasons in MLS, but in 2008 the club was poised to make a change.

Assistant coach Robin Fraser, who had played alongside Borchers in Colorado, told the center back he wanted him to be a core piece at Real Salt Lake.

As he returned stateside to join Salt Lake, Borchers recognized he needed to find balance in his life.

"I wanted to win trophies," Borchers said. "But I didn't want to be a soccer robot. Having other things to do and a life off the field was really important for me."

In Salt Lake, Borchers found that balance. He quickly adjusted to his new city, earned his real estate license and even started a small real estate company.

On the field, Salt Lake brought in a core group that could be part of the club for years to come. On-field success immediately followed.

In 2008, RSL made it to the conference finals before falling to the New York Red Bulls. A year later, the team overcame all odds to win the MLS Cup.

"I think it was intelligent from RSL to have that spine of players down the middle and have Nat anchoring the group on the back line," Salt Lake defender Tony Beltran said. "You need players that are going to compete game in and game out, and Nat's that type of guy."

With each passing year, Borchers grew more comfortable calling Salt Lake home, so much so that in 2014, when he found out he would be leaving, Borchers broke down in tears.

Still, after deciding to join the Timbers, he also vowed that he would put everything he could into his new club.

"I was absolutely shocked," RSL midfielder Kyle Beckerman said. "I had no idea anything like that would happen to Nat. It's going down right now as one of the worst trades Real Salt Lake has done."

• • •

From the moment he arrived in Portland, it was clear Borchers would be a key piece for the Timbers.

This season, he has brought a consistent veteran pres-

ence to Portland's back line, where he plays alongside English veteran Liam Ridgewell.

Off the field, Borchers has become a fan favorite, with his signature bushy red beard endearing him to Portland fans.

But up until recently, Borchers and his family still felt like they were in Portland on an extended vacation. For months, they avoided unpacking the boxes in their home in Lake Oswego.

All that changed on Aug. 15.

The Timbers were locked in a scoreless draw at Real Salt Lake when they were awarded a corner kick late in stoppage time. Diego Valeri sent the ball into the box and Borchers leapt above the fray, heading it down past the reach of RSL goalkeeper Nick Rimando.

Borchers didn't celebrate. Instead he kneeled down on the pitch and closed his eyes. For years, he had defended RSL's goal at Rio Tinto Stadium, the same field where he had just led his new team to victory. It was one of the toughest and most emotional moments of his career.

But it also brought him closure.

"He was there a long time," Porter said. "It's hard to now switch gears and put on a different uniform and play against that club, but I think it was huge for him to almost put that behind him by playing there and getting the goal."

• • •

On a recent afternoon, Borchers lounged on a couch in his living room watching his son, Lincoln, play with a small Portland Timbers ball. The 14-month-old learned to crawl, then walk, then talk in that Lake Oswego house.

"Over time, we've gotten woven into the fabric of the community a little bit more," Borchers said. "And we've felt more at home."

A few weeks ago, Nat and Crystal finally decided to finish unpacking. In their entryway, they hung a giant log slab, which Borchers received for scoring his first Timbers goal against Dallas in April.

Borchers doesn't spend too much time looking ahead, but, now 34, he recognizes he might end his soccer career in Portland.

And just like he has strived for during his entire career, he wants to make his mark during his time in the Rose City and give something back to the fans and community that have embraced him so quickly.

Right now, he feels like this is where he belongs.

"To be able to win a trophy for the club is an incredible accomplishment for our group and definitely for my career." ∎

LEFT AND OPPOSITE: Nat Borchers celebrates after scoring a goal for the Timbers during the first Western Conference Championship match against FC Dallas at Providence Park on Nov. 22. It would be his only goal of the postseason.

Thomas Boyd/The Oregonian/OregonLive

NAT BORCHERS

Age: 34

Height: 6'2"

Position: Defender

Birthplace: Tucson, Arizona

Nat Borchers Trivia: He played with Landon Donovan on the U.S. Men's National Team in 2005.

2015 Stats

Regular-Season Goals: 3

Regular-Season Blocks: 31

Postseason Goals: 1

Postseason Blocks: 6

Diego Chara: Midfielder logs big minutes as mainstay in Timbers lineup

By Jamie Goldberg

In 2010, Portland Timbers general manager Gavin Wilkinson found himself in Tolima, Colombia, scouting a match between Deportes Tolima and Millonarios Fútbol Club, two of that country's top teams.

Wilkinson was building a roster for the Timbers' first MLS season and as he watched the two teams battle in a close and tense match, his focus turned to a hard-working and consistent defensive midfielder competing for Tolima.

From that moment on, Wilkinson made it his priority to bring Diego Chara to Portland.

"We kept going back to Colombia to watch him play," Wilkinson said. "And we fell in love with him more and more."

When Wilkinson first asked Deportes Tolima officials if Chara would be available, they balked. Later, Tolima asked for an impossibly steep transfer fee. Finally, in 2011, after Tolima had been eliminated from the Copa Libertadores, the most prestigious soccer competition in South America, the Timbers shelled out $2 million between the transfer fee, contract and total compensation to bring Chara to Portland as their first designated player.

It's a move they've never regretted.

Since arriving in 2011, Chara has developed into a mainstay in the Timbers lineup. The midfielder has appeared in 146 matches, starting 145 of those on the

way to compiling 12,835 minutes.

But Chara's value doesn't always show up in the statistics. His energetic presence, professional approach and fearlessness have fueled the Timbers.

"I think if you're looking at a list of the most underrated guys in MLS, he's got to be up there," Timbers coach Caleb Porter said. "When he's in there, we don't lose very much."

• • •

As soon as Diego could walk, he started spending his afternoons in the street outside his home in Cali, Colombia, a barefoot child kicking a soccer ball back and forth with his father, Jesús, and his two brothers, Yimmy and Luis Felipe.

"My dad was a football player, not a professional, but he was the one who started us in the game," Chara said through an interpreter. "He taught us to love football."

By the time Chara was 4, he and his brothers were

ABOVE: Diego Chara received the Timbers Army fan award after the Timbers beat the Colorado Rapids, 4-1 at Providence Park on Oct. 25. Randy L. Rasmussen/The Oregonian/OregonLive

OPPOSITE: Diego Chara raises the MLS Cup after the Timbers defeated the Columbus Crew in the MLS Cup final at MAPFRE Stadium in Columbus, Ohio, on Dec. 6. Randy L. Rasmussen/The Oregonian/OregonLive

attending a developmental soccer school called "Las Ceibas." From there, Chara started playing for Boca Juniors de Cali and then joined the youth ranks of Deportes Quindio, a club that plays in Colombia's top league.

At 18, Chara started competing for the senior club. He would make 124 appearances with Deportes Quindio over four years, drawing the attention of some of the top clubs in Colombia in the process.

"We really didn't know that we were going to become professional soccer players," Chara said. "The one thing that we knew is we loved the game. It's what I've always felt I could do best."

Chara's brothers also rose through the pro soccer ranks. Luis Felipe competed for a number of Colombian teams before heading to Venezuela to play for Aragua Fútbol Club. Yimmy played in Colombia's second division before moving on to play with Diego, who by then was competing for Deportes Tolima.

And on that fateful day in 2010, Wilkinson watched the skilled and fearless 24-year-old dart around the field with confidence and offered him a chance to leave Colombia for the United States.

"I hadn't really thought about going to the United States and MLS, but it was an opportunity that came up," Chara said. "When I started thinking about it, I thought it was just going to be a good decision for my future — for my career, my life and my family."

• • •

When Chara arrived in Portland, he didn't speak a word of English.

He laughs when he recalls former Timbers coach John Spencer yelling out commands in his thick Scottish brogue during those first months of training. Spencer spoke fast, Chara said. He never understood a word his coach said.

"It was hard, but we had a person who helped translate in practice," Chara said. "At the end of the day, when you get in the game, it's easy. Football is football."

Since Chara isn't a goal scorer, it's often hard to quantify his impact.

He is often at the center of key plays and consistently covers more ground than anybody else on the field, an ability that allows him to both prevent counterattacks when his team turns the ball over and launch attacks on offense.

"I just see it and I go for it," Chara said. "I've always been like that since I was 4 years old."

Porter called Chara a perfect "modern" box-to-box midfielder. Every team wants a midfielder who has the intangible skills to screen the back line, disrupt the other team and win balls.

And Chara is incredibly effective in his nuanced role, Porter said. The Timbers coach believes Chara is one of the best ball winners in the league.

"He shows up every day, does his job and has a great attitude," Porter said. "He doesn't need credit. At the end of the day, he wants to win, that's it." ∎

OPPOSITE: Diego Chara kicks the ball against the New York Red Bulls on Sept. 20 at Providence Park. Chara played in 28 games in 2015, subbing out of only two of those games.

Thomas Boyd/The Oregonian/OregonLive

LEFT: FC Dallas forward Tesho Akindele and Timbers midfielder Diego Chara eye the ball while trying for position during the MLS Western Conference Championship game at Toyota Stadium in Frisco, Texas, on Nov. 29. Chara would draw a warning in this game. He led the Timbers in yellow cards with eight during the 2015 season.

Stewart F. House/The Oregonian/OregonLive

OPPOSITE: Diego Chara intercepts the ball against the Vancouver Whitecaps on July 18 at Providence Park. Chara was named Player of the Year in 2015 by both the Timbers players and Timbers supporters.

Thomas Boyd/The Oregonian/OregonLive

DIEGO CHARA

Age: 29
Height: 5'8"
Position: Midfielder
Birthplace: Cali, Colombia
Diego Chara Trivia: Chara led the Timbers in yellow cards with eight.

2015 Stats
Regular-Season Goals: 2
Regular-Season Assists: 1
Postseason Goals: 0
Postseason Assists: 1

Alvas Powell: With mother's encouragement, young star rises to prominence

By Jamie Goldberg

Angella Powell stood outside the door to her home in the remote eastern part of Jamaica, sweeping away dust from the doorstep as she waited anxiously for her son, Alvas, to return home.

When she finally saw him walking up to the house, she paused expectantly.

There on the doorstep, Alvas Powell told his mother that he had received his visa and would be leaving Jamaica and the town where he grew up to play professional soccer for the Portland Timbers more than 3,000 miles away.

Angella immediately dropped her broom and wrapped her arms tightly around her son. They stood together outside for a long time that day in June 2013, as Angella sobbed into the 18-year-old's shoulder.

Powell had never visited the United States, and neither son nor mother had ever heard of Portland. But ever since he was a youngster, Powell had shown immense soccer talent and, with his mother's unwavering support, fought to move up the ranks in Jamaica in hopes of fulfilling his unlikely wish of one day playing pro soccer abroad.

He finally had a chance to make his dream a reality.

• • •

Danvers Pen is a small farming community in south-eastern Jamaica, a humble town of about 1,500 in St. Thomas, where more than 32 percent of the population lives in abject poverty.

This is where Angella Powell raised her seven children, even after their stepfather left her, working as a domestic worker cleaning houses and washing clothes to support her large family.

"I didn't have a perfect job," Angella said. "I would do washing and cleaning for people, whatever I could. The money wasn't great, but I just pushed on. It was really rough on me, really rough."

Despite the struggles, Angella worked fiercely to provide for her children, especially her only son, Alvas, the third youngest.

Even while he was in primary school, it was clear that Alvas was athletically gifted. He would run track — the sport that has earned Jamaica international recognition — and always come home with medals.

But it was on the soccer field that Alvas found his calling.

"He started playing in primary school and I would go to every game," Angella said. "I didn't miss a match. I knew back then that he was very good. I knew he was going to reach his goals. He was meant to make it."

His talent was impossible to overlook. By age 9, he was competing for a local club and, as he moved into his teenage years, he started getting noticed by teams throughout Jamaica, as well as the national team program.

"Growing up it was not easy for me or any other kid in my community," Powell said. "There are no opportunities. You have to fight for what you want."

Powell's talent and hard work earned him a call-up to the U-17 Jamaican National Team at the age of 16. But making it at the highest level would cost money and require significant travel.

He told his mother he would forgo the opportunity and stay in Danvers Pen, but she told him he had to chase his dream.

"My mom is a big part of my life," Powell said. "No matter what, she sacrificed herself just to give me things because I didn't have a father there. My mom is my father and mother in one, so she played a big part in my life growing up."

Powell went on to represent Jamaica at the 2011 FIFA U-17 World Cup, before finally making his debut with the senior national team in 2012. That same year, he joined Portmore United FC, which plays in the Jamaica National Premier League.

The young and raw right back made just 10 appearances with Portmore before the Portland Timbers, who had seen Powell play for the Jamaican National Team, offered the teenager an opportunity to come to the United States on a loan deal.

"When he left, I cried one whole week because I missed him," Angella said. "But every day I calmed down and I told myself, 'This is what he needs to be doing.' I had no idea what Portland was about or what it was like, but in my faith I knew it must be somewhere good."

• • •

During his first few weeks in Portland, Powell just wanted to go home.

The Timbers' youngest player was soft-spoken and shy, and had trouble mustering up the confidence to talk to his new teammates. He would quietly attend practices, then shower and leave as quickly as possibly, scurrying home to his apartment in Southwest Portland to call his family back home.

But fellow Jamaicans Donovan Ricketts and Ryan Johnson, and African players Pa Modou Kah and Futty Danso were quick to take Powell under their wings. Kah would often try to force Powell to talk in the locker room, hoping to help the teenager overcome his shyness.

And playing in a soccer-crazed city like Portland made adjusting to the Timbers easier.

On Aug. 3, 2013, when the Timbers returned home to Providence Park after two games on the road, Portland coach Caleb Porter decided to give Powell his first start in a Timbers uniform.

As he stepped onto the pitch that night and looked up at the waves of frenzied fans in the stands, Powell was overwhelmed.

Just months before, he had been playing at a local sports complex in Jamaica, where it was considered a stroke of good fortune when fans decided to attend games, and the referees sometimes failed to show up when it rained. Now, he looked up at the crowded stands, some 20,000 strong, where fans stood chanting rhythmically as they waved handmade flags above their heads.

"I had a lot of goose bumps," Powell said. "It was just unbelievable. I thought I was dreaming."

Powell started just four games in 2013 before Porter decided to use a veteran back line to stabilize the defense down the stretch and lead the Timbers into the MLS playoffs.

Still, the Timbers saw immense promise and potential in Powell and brought him back again on loan in 2014.

"We were bringing him into Portland not as a starter, but as someone we could develop into a starter," Timbers general manager Gavin Wilkinson said.

Early in 2014, Powell saw some playing time for the Timbers and even had a few opportunities in the starting 11.

But the right back still had a lot to learn. That became abundantly clear May 17 when he took a heavy touch against the Columbus Crew and tried to recover by making a late and reckless tackle on Crew defender Chad Barson. Barson went flying. Powell was issued a red card and dejectedly walked off the field with his head down.

Soon after, Powell was on a flight to Sacramento to join the Timbers USL PRO affiliate, the Sacramento Republic, on loan.

"I thought that was important to send him on loan because he needed to, in some ways, appreciate the opportunity that he had here and he needed to see the other side of what could happen if he didn't make it here," Porter said. "He needed something to wake him up a little bit."

• • •

Powell's loan to Sacramento didn't go quite as planned.

The young defender felt isolated and unhappy in California's capital and he struggled on the field. Powell made just two appearances for the Republic before they decided that he wasn't going to fit into their starting lineup. They ultimately told the Timbers that they were sending him back to Portland.

Shortly after returning to the Rose City, Powell met with Porter to discuss the loan stint. The Timbers coach was frank.

"Hey, listen, that didn't go that well," Porter says he told him. "So, what are you going to do now?"

Porter was talking to a much more mature Powell. Even though he had struggled in Sacramento, he had returned with a newfound determination.

"I realized that I don't want to go back home to Jamaica and sit around and do nothing," Powell said. "I want something from this. I want to prove that I deserve to be on this team, I deserve to be starting."

In practice, Powell began to concentrate more intently on his coach's directions. He had always been athletic, with explosive speed, but now Powell started focusing on his defense. His one-on-one defending quickly improved as he learned to stay focused and composed.

Soon Powell found himself in the starting lineup.

A stretch of impressive performances in late 2014 earned him a multiyear deal to stay in Portland. He's been a mainstay in the starting 11 ever since.

"He's grown a lot over the last couple of years," Timbers veteran Jack Jewsbury said. "You see now, he's a threat game in and game out."

Although Powell still shows his youth at times, he has grown into a talented and consistent starter, and the Timbers believe he has the potential to grow into

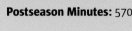

ALVAS POWELL

Age: 21
Height: 6'0"
Position: Defender
Birthplace: Danvers Pen, St. Thomas, Jamaica
Alvas Powell Trivia: He played every minute of the MLS Cup Playoffs.

2015 Stats
Regular-Season Starts: 31
Regular-Season Minutes: 2,726
Postseason Starts: 6
Postseason Minutes: 570

an even more dangerous player.

"I think Alvas is starting to make a statement as one of the better, most complete right backs in MLS," Porter said.

• • •

Angella Powell keeps a collection of photos of her son playing for the Timbers that hang on the wall in her home back in Jamaica. Sometimes, she will wake up in the middle of the night and stare at the photos, a smile beaming across her face.

Even though she rarely sees him anymore, the bond between mother and son has never wavered. Angella speaks to Powell over the phone daily — she says she can't go any longer than a day without hearing his voice. And Powell has never lost sight of his roots, either. He sends part of his paycheck home to support his mom, helping her just as she supported him along the way. She recently received her visa and hopes to finally make an extended trip to visit her son in Portland and see him play.

"I tell him, 'I'm not around you, but do your best,'" Angella said. "'The whole world is watching you.'" ■

LEFT: Alvas Powell works against a Vancouver Whitecaps defender during the Western Conference semifinal match on Nov. 1 at Providence Park. Thomas Boyd/The Oregonian/OregonLive

Adam Kwarasey: Goalkeeper finds his voice on and off the field

By Molly Blue

When his turn came, Adam Kwarasey didn't hesitate.

The Portland Timbers goalkeeper took four strides, loaded up a solid leg swing and shot the ball past Sporting Kansas City goalkeeper Jon Kempin, who had no chance to stop it.

When the pressure was on Kempin, Kwarasey again didn't hesitate. He took his place on the line and dove right to stop Kempin's shot, giving the Timbers a dramatic win in an 11-round penalty kick shootout in the knockout round of the Major League Soccer Cup playoffs.

When he realized what he'd done, and before his teammates could swarm him, Kwarasey surrendered the cool, calm exterior Timbers fans have come to know. He pumped his fist before leaping into the frenzied scrum on the field in the midst of a Providence Park-rocking celebration.

"He's cool, calm and collected, even reserved in many ways," Timbers general manager Gavin Wilkinson said in a recent interview, "But he's got emotion."

It was a signature moment in a season filled with big games for Kwarasey, his first with the Timbers, who spotted him in 2013 and liked what they saw.

"We have a lot of confidence in Adam," Wilkinson said. "That's one of the things about him. He's very confident, very composed."

Kwarasey, 27, was playing for Strømsgodset in the Norwegian Tippeligaen until last season. He'd been named goalkeeper of the year in 2013, backstopping Strømsgodset to the league title. The son of a Norwegian mother and Ghanian father, he has 23 caps for Ghana, dating back to 2011 and as recently as the 2014 World Cup.

After eight seasons with Strømsgodset, Kwarasey was ready to make a move when the Timbers approached him before the 2015 season. They were looking to make a change and he was looking for a new challenge.

"I wanted to challenge myself. I wanted to get better," Kwarasey said.

Wilkinson said that with Kwarasey, "there was a lot of homework done." By the time they all sat down together, Wilkinson was convinced that Kwarasey "did tick all the boxes."

For his part, Kwarasey said it was "cool" when the Timbers began to scout him. He didn't know much about the team or the community, but he did his research and saw a fit.

The Timbers and Kwarasey came to terms in late 2014, and he packed up his family, including his girlfriend, Malin Feldt, and their infant son Elijah, and headed to Portland. In the Rose City he found a community filled with contrasts, from the nearby coast and the mountains to nature parks and urban bustle, all ready for them to explore.

He adapted — and was adopted — quickly.

Kwarasey was honored at the end of the regular season as the Timbers' Community Player of the Year, working with Special Olympics Oregon, the Children's Cancer Association and the Cascadia Unified Challenge through the club's Stand Together program.

But on the field, the transition was a bit bumpy.

The Timbers, looking to shore up a leaky defense after the 2014 season, also had brought in veteran defender Nat Borchers from Real Salt Lake to play alongside Liam Ridgewell, Jorge Villafana and Alvas Powell. Behind the back line, Kwarasey helped plug the holes, even if it took a little time.

"It's been challenging for me to get to know everybody quickly and also try to perform," Kwarasey said. "It took a couple of months just to get used to everything."

Everything. From a team of new faces to a home in a new country, Kwarasey said that the adjustments

---

ADAM KWARASEY

Age: 27

Height: 6'3"

Position: Goalkeeper

Birthplace: Oslo, Norway

Adam Kawarsey Trivia: He's made 23 appearances for the Ghana National Team, including one start during the 2014 World Cup.

2015 Stats

Regular-Season Shutouts: 13

Regular-Season Saves: 80

Postseason Shutouts: 1

Postseason Saves: 9

weren't always easy after playing so long in his native Norway.

"It's my first time playing abroad. MLS is just different than what I'm used to in Europe," he said.

But he's found his voice and it blends well with the defense in front of him. He's soft-spoken off the field, but his teammates hear him just fine when pressure builds in a game.

"I communicate a lot with my back four," Kwarasey said "We're keeping everyone on their toes." ■

LEFT: Adam Kwarasey reacts after a penalty kick during the shootout against Sporting Kansas City at Providence Park on Oct. 29. The Timbers beat Sporting Kansas City 7-6 on penalty kicks in a knockout game after the two clubs played to a 2-2 draw over 120 minutes of regulation time before 21,144 fans. It was Kwarasey who converted Portland's last penalty kick before stopping an attempt by Kansas City goalkeeper Jon Kempin.
Randy L. Rasmussen/The Oregonian/OregonLive

OPPOSITE: The Timbers Army unveils an Adam Kwarasey tifo that reads "The power of Kwarasey stops you hosers" to honor the Timbers goalkeeper before the Timbers' MLS Cup Playoffs game against the Vancouver Whitecaps at Providence Park on Nov. 1.
Thomas Boyd/The Oregonian/OregonLive

THE COACH

ABOVE: Timbers head coach Caleb Porter flashes a No. 1 sign to fans attending the Western Conference Championship match against FC Dallas at Toyota Stadium in Frisco, Texas, on Nov. 29. Stewart F. House/The Oregonian/OregonLive

OPPOSITE: Coach Caleb Porter was relaxed on the sidelines before the team played Orlando City SC on April 12 at Providence Park. Thomas Boyd/The Oregonian/OregonLive

Caleb Porter: Tour of coach's 'museum' reveals man on a mission

By John Canzano

The home office in Caleb Porter's house contains a glass-topped desk with a parenting book sitting on it. He's positioned the desk facing both a television where he can watch film of his Timbers and the front window so he can watch his children ride their bicycles while he works. His walls and shelves are covered with mementos, including framed jerseys from a couple of his former college players, a scarf from his national championship run at the University of Akron and photographs from their visits to the White House.

The Adidas cleats Porter last wore as a college player in 1997 sit on a shelf – laces still tied – frozen in time. A determined and sentimental Porter pried his feet out after his final game at Indiana.

This is a nostalgic man. The master curator, who knows the story of every framed scrap. But it's what's absent from the one-room Caleb Porter Museum that strikes you.

The coach of the Portland Timbers refuses to display anything from the franchise. Not a photo. Not a scarf. Not a splinter or stitch. In fact, Porter says his MLS assistants, his general manager and even Timbers' owner Merritt Paulson have never even seen the room.

"When you start putting stuff up you're done and retired," the Timbers' coach said. "I have a closet of stuff I've saved, but I'll put it up in 20 years when I'm done here."

• • •

Porter and his wife, Andrea, have three children under 7, two boys and a girl. When the kids arrive home from school with mom on Wednesday, they rumble through the garage door of their Lake Oswego home. Then, they peek down the hallway to see if dad is in his office. His youngest, a girl age 3, is named Stella. She climbs her dad like a playground jungle gym as he gives a wide-ranging and candid interview.

"I never learned to enjoy it," Porter said of the 50 straight victories he once posted as a college coach. "I enjoy it more now when we win. I know how hard it is to win. I know how difficult wins are to come by.

"I had to learn to lose games."

When Porter, now 40, left Akron for Portland in 2012 Seattle Sounders coach Sigi Schmid offered advice. The successful former UCLA coach said to Porter, "Get used to losing."

"I was like, 'What does that mean?' Was he taunting me? Was he telling me he was going to beat me?" Porter said. "I didn't get it then, but I get it now. I understand what Sigi was saying. You win and win and win in college, then you come to the pros and if you don't know how to lose you'll go crazy."

Porter dissolves in thought somewhere else in that moment. His mind is centered on Oct. 30, 2010. He has a gifted pupil and teenager named Darlington Nagbe on the Akron squad. That Zips powerhouse hadn't lost a match in more than two calendar years when it visited a Cleveland State team that was 6-9 at the time.

Akron got beat 2-1.

"I didn't even address my team after the game. I just made them get on the bus," Porter said. "I thought it was the end of the world. When we got off the bus I gathered them behind closed doors and I lost it.

"I went ballistic."

ABOVE AND LEFT: Timbers coach Caleb Porter lives in Lake Oswego with wife Andrea and three children under 7, including Stella, 3. Beth Nakamura/The Oregonian/OregonLive

OPPOSITE: Caleb Porter holds the last pair of cleats he wore as a college player, with the laces still tied.

Beth Nakamura/The Oregonian/OregonLive

One of the jerseys displayed in Porter's office is Nagbe's college jersey from that season. Below that on the wall there is a framed tribute to the Zips victory over Louisville in the NCAA championship match. Porter's game plan "set pieces" are printed on a couple of sheets of paper, framed there. He stops talking, studies them, and finally says, "I can't believe I won a championship with those primitive set pieces.

"It's like I didn't know what I was doing."

• • •

The cleaning ladies that the Porter family hired come on Wednesdays, every other week. Early in the season, with the Timbers struggling, one of them was dusting his office when she accidentally bumped a Tiffany & Co. crystal on the mantel.

It fell on the tile in front of the fireplace and shattered.

"I still have all the pieces," Andrea Porter said.

That crystal was her husband's 2013 MLS Coach of the Year award. She called Tiffany & Co. and they wanted $800 to make a replacement trophy.

"I'm just not the kind of guy who is going to pay $800 to replace an award," Caleb Porter said. "I thought it was a sign. I'm such a symbolic guy it bothered me, but then I realized it's just a way of telling me that that stuff is meaningless. Good coaches don't coach for awards."

Porter said he went through a shift after his hiring by Paulson. Prior to the 2015 season Porter studied Chelsea FC and its then coach José Mourinho. Porter plotted to ambush the MLS. He was going to play a style unseen before in American soccer, aggressive and attacking.

"We were going to press, and attack, and be aggressive like nobody else," he said. "And it sometimes worked. But also, we got caught. We were out of balance. We were impatient. We forced things. We didn't play mature and we paid for it. Looking back, I realized I overdid it. That was on me."

Porter said this Timbers team is now more measured in style.

ABOVE: Caleb Porter raises a scarf after the Timbers beat the Colorado Rapids 4-1 at Providence Park on Oct. 25. Randy L. Rasmussen/The Oregonian/OregonLive

LEFT: Caleb Porter talks with Lucas Melano on the sidelines during the match against the New York Red Bulls on Sept. 20 at Providence Park. Thomas Boyd/The Oregonian/OregonLive

FAR LEFT: Caleb Porter watches game action against Orlando City SC on April 12 at Providence Park. Thomas Boyd/The Oregonian/OregonLive

"We attack and we are aggressive, but we're pragmatic about it. We lacked that before. You have to be pragmatic."

Porter believes the soccer he's seen in the last month is in balance.

"We're better than we've ever been right now."

• • •

During the long break before the Western Conference finals, Porter tried to stay busy.

He and Andrea, who was also a soccer player at Indiana, attended the Blazers home game against the Spurs early this season. They watched the first half of the return of LaMarcus Aldridge with friends before grabbing a cocktail on the club level at halftime. Porter sipped his drink and talked about how badly he wanted to bottle the Timbers' momentum. He wondered how he'd keep from going nuts waiting for kickoff, and revealed that he'd planned to give his team a rest instead of pushing hard through the long break.

"I've made that mistake before," he said.

Caleb does all the family cooking with the barbecue on their deck. He cooks the meat, Andrea prepares the side dishes. The Porter house is surrounded in their neighborhood by Nike executives, not far from Lakeridge High. Caleb lowers his voice, begins pointing at the houses around him, marking the surrounding Swooshes.

He says: "I've always been an Adidas guy."

A guy who happens to be keeping busy this week by seeing a movie with his wife. The couple watched Matt Damon in "The Martian." Porter said he relates to Damon's character (Mark Watney), stranded on Mars, alone, and with nothing to do but figure things out or die trying.

"All alone, left for dead – that's coaching," Porter said. "It's a lonely business. You have to get yourself up out of the dirt and focus on the process. It's problem solving and creative engineering. Also, for a coach, it doesn't end well. You get fired. So you might as well do it your way."

• • •

In the home office there's a framed photograph on a table of a toddler in a pair of blue overalls sitting on a log. It's young Caleb Porter, then just a tow-headed kid living in Spokane. Before the family moved to Michigan, Porter's father was a logger in Washington.

"I feel like sometimes things come around in a circle for a reason," Porter said. "Like a direction of your life doesn't make any sense, then all of a sudden, everything comes together. It's like you just go with it, and then everything makes sense.

"That photo is one of those reminders to me."

Porter is a disciple of former IU coach Jerry Yeagley, the most successful collegiate coach in history. Across the room, a framed mural of Yeagley hangs over the fireplace, in center position. It's the Mona Lisa here.

"If college soccer is college basketball," Porter said, "Yeagley is John Wooden."

On the fireplace mantel below there's two more framed photographs. On the left side, a photo of the 2010 championship celebration by Akron. Porter is getting a Gatorade bath. On the right side, a photograph of Porter, hand over heart, coach of the 2010 Men's U.S. National team. That team failed to make the Olympic tournament.

Career highlight to the left. Career nightmare to the right.

"You don't get all the players, and you don't get some of them for the time period you'd like," he said. "I didn't realize all the challenges of that national team experience.

"I failed."

The curator won't say if he wants another shot someday.

• • •

The former mayor of Akron is a guy named Donald Plusquellic. He told Caleb Porter once during a city ceremony that only two people have been honored with keys to the city: One is Porter, the other, LeBron James.

Porter held the key and said, "I don't know if that's true or not, but that's a pretty cool thing to say. I also

don't know what you're supposed to do with a key. Do I wear it around my neck? Or what?"

Porter is a romantic. He's nostalgic. He's a collector of memories and forever in search of meaning, especially if there's a good story or a hint of poetry involved. In a few days, his team would begin the biggest series in the MLS-era of Timbers soccer, with its best chance to break through.

He's played with the children (Stella, Jake, 5, and Colin, 7). He's gone on date nights. He's read books, and seen movies, and cooked dinner. Now, Porter pulls you from artifact to artifact, directing a tour designed to shorten the wait to kick. But soon enough, there would be a game to coach, and he'll wake up, face down on Mars, with creative engineering to be done.

Before the tour ends, Porter stops cold.

He wants you to see two thin slips of paper he's saved all season under a paperweight on his desk. He holds them up. They're messages from inside fortune cookies. He received them earlier this season when the Timbers were struggling and Porter needed a lift.

The first message reads: "Today's preparation determines tomorrow's achievement."

The second is printed with: "You'll be called upon to celebrate good news."

Porter points out how uplifting the messages are. Then, he thinks for a moment.

"I guess every fortune cookie message is positive," he said. "I guess what I'm really saying is that when you're down, eat Chinese food." ∎

SOCCER CITY, USA

ABOVE: Fans in the Timbers Army section at Providence Park wave flags and cheer before the first leg of the Portland Timbers' Western Conference Championship matchup against FC Dallas on Nov. 22.

Thomas Boyd/The Oregonian/OregonLive

OPPOSITE: Portland Timbers fans erupt following a goal scored by their team during an MLS Cup Playoffs knockout round game against Sporting Kansas City on Oct. 29 at Providence Park.

Randy L. Rasmussen/The Oregonian/OregonLive

Timbers Army capos orchestrate show at Providence Park

By Jamie Goldberg

The singing in the north end of Providence Park began to slow as Diego Valeri's cross floated into the box. In the stands, all eyes got wider and fans held their collective breaths as they intently watched the arc of the ball.

Even before Lucas Melano raised his foot to the ball and redirected it into the net, Patch Perryman knew it was going to be a goal.

He could see it in the eyes of the fans.

"The lead up to a goal is pretty intense when you're watching the game on the pitch," Perryman said. "But imagine for just a moment that you're watching that lead up to a goal unfold through hundreds and thousands of eyes. It's a unique experience."

Perryman is an integral part of a small and dedicated group of capos that spend each and every Portland Timbers match standing on raised platforms in the north end of Providence Park as they lead the Timbers Army in song.

Capos are not unique to Portland, but the Timbers Army capos play a critical role in creating a distinctive and awe-inspiring atmosphere at Providence Park. Throughout the game, they act as conductors, keeping the crowd on its feet and singing in unison from the opening minute until well after the final whistle.

"When people talk about the Timbers, the first thing they talk about is the Timbers Army," said Camden Murray, who has been a capo since 2009 and now serves as the lead capo at the foot of Section 107. "We all have our own individual roles in the Timbers Army family and mine is being a capo."

When Murray started attending Timbers games in 2006, the crowd was much smaller and the job of a capo was much less formalized. At each game, a constantly changing procession of capos would stand atop milk crates as they tried to lead the crowd in England-style pub songs.

But as the Timbers Army swelled, they adopted more original chants and their game day traditions became more ritualized. Soon it became necessary to have a group of official capos spread along the north end to keep the crowd in sync and as vociferous and energized as possible.

LEFT: Portland Timbers mascot Timber Joey holds a slab aloft following a goal scored in the Timbers' 4-1 victory over the Colorado Rapids at Providence Park on Oct. 25.
Randy L. Rasmussen/The Oregonian/OregonLive

OPPOSITE: Fans in the Timbers Army section at Providence Park celebrate a goal scored against the rival Seattle Sounders with green smoke and the unfurling of their traditional "Big Ass Flag" on June 28. Randy L. Rasmussen/The Oregonian/OregonLive

"It was more organic and less choreographed for the most part before the Timbers went to MLS," said Rob Frisina, a capo who has been attending games since 2008. "There is a much stronger need to have consistency with so many fans and with the sections so far apart now, but we also have the opportunity to create a unique atmosphere."

The game day environment at Providence Park is renowned throughout MLS due in large part to the organic atmosphere that the Timbers Army creates. But getting a group of more than 1,000 fans to sing and dance in unison throughout the match is hardly an easy task.

At certain points in the game, the Timbers Army

has set songs – like singing "You Are My Sunshine" at the 80th minute or "Can't Help Falling in Love" at the 85th minute – but during the rest of the match it is the job of the capos to put together a set list that

ABOVE: A Timbers Army capo leads cheers in the north end of Providence Park during a scoreless draw against Real Salt Lake on March 7. Thomas Boyd/The Oregonian/OregonLive

OPPOSITE: Timbers fans cheer their team through a haze of green smoke following a goal scored by midfielder Diego Chara against FC Dallas on April 4. Thomas Boyd/The Oregonian/OregonLive

harmonizes with the play on the field.

Murray is the capo tasked with picking each song. He tries to turn away from the crowd and take in enough of the game to pick appropriate tunes. When he's settled on a song, he uses hand signals to convey to the rest of the capos and the drums and trumpets which song is coming next.

"We are trying to set the beat for the match and cater to the match with our songs," Murray said. "We want to create a soundtrack to the match that's appropriate, but we also try to push the match forward with our songs rather than just react to the match."

Being a capo comes with immense sense of pride.

Even though it's difficult for the capos to take in games in any traditional sense, they recognize that they are helping to drive something much bigger.

Players throughout MLS talk about performing in front of the Timbers Army and when the thunderous chants from the north end fill the stadium, especially late in games as the Timbers are pushing for a win, the capos believe that the groundswell of songs can have a real impact on the game.

"There's something going on in the north end that affects what's going on in the game and all the other teams know it," Perryman said. "To be a small part of that, to be helping to push that energy where it's going to be most effective is a good feeling." ■

ABOVE: A Timbers Army tifo reads "WE'RE GONNA RIDE THIS BULL ALL THE WAY" behind the "Cup bound and down" playoffs slogan and an image of Kenny Powers riding a bull before the first leg of the Timbers' MLS Cup Playoffs match against FC Dallas at Providence Park on Nov. 22. Thomas Boyd/The Oregonian/OregonLive

LEFT: Timber Joey presents a log slab to the crowd as the sun sets behind Providence Park during a game against the Vancouver Whitecaps on July 18. Thomas Boyd/The Oregonian/OregonLive

OPPOSITE TOP: With his chainsaw in hand, Timber Joey peeks over his shoulder to get a look at the action on the pitch during the Portland Timbers' Western Conference Championship game against FC Dallas at Providence Park on Nov. 22. Thomas Boyd/The Oregonian/OregonLive

OPPOSITE BOTTOM: The watch party crowd that packed into the Crystal Ballroom in Portland erupts after the Timbers scored their first goal in an MLS Cup Playoffs away game against FC Dallas on Nov. 29.

Stephanie Yao Long/The Oregonian/OregonLive

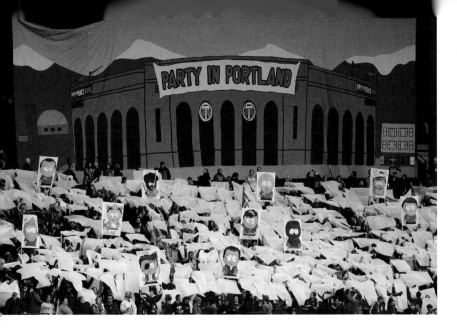

ABOVE: The Timbers Army unveils a "Party in Portland" tifo with a South Park theme before a game against the Colorado Rapids at Providence Park on Oct. 25. Randy L. Rasmussen/The Oregonian/OregonLive

ABOVE RIGHT: A Timbers Army capo waves a giant checkered flag as fans celebrate a Timbers goal scored during the first leg of Portland's Western Conference Championship match against FC Dallas in the MLS Cup Playoffs at Providence Park on Nov. 22.

Thomas Boyd/The Oregonian/OregonLive

RIGHT: A fan hoists a Timbers Army scarf during the Portland Timbers' 4-1 win over the Colorado Rapids on Oct. 25.

Randy L. Rasmussen/The Oregonian/OregonLive

OPPOSITE: Fans in the north end of Providence Park celebrate a goal scored by defender Nat Borchers in a game against FC Dallas on April 4. Thomas Boyd/The Oregonian/OregonLive

A fan's 40-year love affair with the Portland Timbers

By Jamie Goldberg

From his perch at the top of the L in the Key Club section of Providence Park, Adam Lewis often gazes out at the Timbers Army as they throw up their scarves in unison during the Star-Spangled Banner.

In those moments, the memories come flooding back.

Lewis recalls watching Portland Timbers games with his parents and sister, Jenny, from the north end in what was then section 217. Of course, that was long before the renovations, when the park was still known as Civic Stadium and was primarily used as a baseball field.

Back then, security was lax, and before games an 11-year-old Lewis would often walk down onto the field to hang homemade butcher paper banners on the outfield wall.

"I'm so grateful we still have that original stadium," says Lewis, 52. "I have all those memories – the way it smells, the color of the paint, the wood cover in the north end. I have 40 years of soccer memories and stories from that stadium."

• • •

The love affair started in 1975.

Adam's father, Paul Lewis, had discovered that Portland would be getting its own soccer team through an article in The Oregonian. The Portland Timbers would be joining the North American Soccer League, the top-level professional soccer league in the United States at the time. The NASL was the first professional soccer league to see success nationally in the United States.

Paul knew very little about the exotic sport, but figured the new attraction would be a fun and inexpensive way to spend some more time with his kids.

The Lewis family missed the Timbers' home opener in 1975, but when the second game came along, Paul decided to bring the family.

The moment Adam entered the stadium, he was struck by the tangible buzz of excitement.

"I looked forward to those games all week long," Adam says. "I can remember hoping that the game would go into overtime sometimes just so there'd be a little more of a game, a little bit longer."

After that first match, Adam didn't miss a single game. He started clipping out everything he could find about the Timbers and began to form a collection of ticket stubs, scarves and other paraphernalia.

After games, Adam and his family would go to either the Benson or Hilton for the Timbers' postgame party. All the players would be there, mingling with fans. Adam would walk around the ballroom nabbing autographs.

It didn't take long before Adam started playing soccer as well. For a while, he would just kick a tetherball around the yard. It still had the knob where a string had once been attached. It would bounce around at random angles. His parents finally gave in and bought him a real soccer ball.

Both Adam and his sister started attending camps run by the Timbers players. After one camp, Adam's sister somehow convinced Timbers winger Willie Anderson to come by the family's house.

"He came by and had a beer with my family and chatted for a little while and left," Adam says. "You just don't see that in a lot of other sports."

• • •

It wasn't easy to follow the Timbers back then. The games weren't on television and were sparingly picked up on the radio. They weren't well covered in the newspapers at all.

Once, when the team traveled to Washington, D.C., to face the Washington Diplomats, the Lewis family found the rare hotel on Sandy Boulevard with a satellite dish. Adam, his sister, parents and grandparents rented a room in the hotel for three hours to watch the game.

Back in the '70s, the Lewis family owned a Volkswagen bus that featured yellow wheels. It was decked out in Timbers gear. They would take the bus to games in Seattle and Vancouver and they would drive down Interstate 5 to the Bay Area and Los Angeles. They once flew all the way to Hawaii for a match.

"We fell in love with it right away," says Paul, who is now 75. "It was just amazing. It's a game you can easily understand, and it takes a lot of skill."

After losing the first match in 1975, the Timbers proceeded to go undefeated at home for the rest of the season.

The Lewis family had missed that first loss. So, as the team headed into the playoffs, Adam was sure they would win the Soccer Bowl. He had no idea what it looked like to see the Timbers lose.

The family went down to Civic Stadium to wait in the long line of fans trying to secure playoff seats. When they were about 10th in line, they learned that there were no tickets left.

They were about to leave when Portland City Commissioner Mildred Schwab came outside the stadium to tell fans to hold tight. The city was working with the fire department to add more seats by putting bleachers

OPPOSITE: As Barry Powell looks on, teammate Brian Godfrey jumps over a sliding Alan Stephens of the Seattle Sounders in the first game of the Portland Timbers' inaugural season on May 5, 1975.
Brent Wojahn/The Oregonian/OregonLive

on the field for the game.

As they waited, Timbers coach Vic Crowe sent the team out to do a victory lap around the stadium.

"I remember climbing up a light pole and giving the players high fives as they went by," Adam says. "That was a really great moment."

• • •

Portland hosted their perennial arch rivals, the Seattle Sounders, in the first round of the playoffs and over 31,000 fans packed into Civic Stadium.

The game went into sudden-death overtime tied at 1-1.

The Timbers were awarded a corner kick during overtime. Anderson set the ball into the baseball dirt on the corner of the field, before sending the ball into the box. It bounced around and was finally passed back to Anderson, who sent another cross into the box.

Timbers forward Tony Betts leaped toward the ball.

From the stands, it felt like slow motion to Adam. Betts got his head on the ball and Adam knew it was going in.

The crowd erupted and fans poured over the north end wall and onto the field to celebrate the 2-1 victory.

Five days later, the Timbers beat the St. Louis Stars in the semifinals and the Lewis family made the drive down to San Jose in their Volkswagen bus for the Soccer Bowl between the Timbers and Tampa Bay Rowdies.

Lewis saw his first Timbers' loss as Portland fell 2-0 to the Rowdies, but the Timbers' success in the 1975 season ignited a base of soccer fans in Portland that has carried through to today.

• • •

The NASL Timbers folded in 1982, two years before the league itself folded.

Adam read the news in The Oregonian. It was one of

the few Timbers articles he didn't cut out.

"I was just crushed," Adam says. "I couldn't believe there was going to be a world without a Portland Timbers team anymore."

The Timbers were briefly reborn as a semi-pro team in the 1980s, but the new age for the club really began in 2001 when the Timbers joined the A-League. The club continued to play in various second tier leagues until they made the move to MLS in 2011.

"It was one of the most amazing things in my adult life," Adam says, "to realize that we were actually going to have a professional soccer team again in Portland."

In the 2000s, Adam got the idea to bring his godson Jesse Fordyce to games. He hoped that Jesse would fall in love with the Timbers, just as he had.

Jesse was seven when Adam took him to his first game as a birthday present. He was immediately hooked.

After Jesse's second game, Adam carried him on his

shoulders down to the field. Jesse met Gavin Wilkinson, who was playing for the Timbers at the time, and asked for his autograph. He still has the autograph hanging in his parents' home in Lake Oswego.

"We knew all the chants," says Jesse, who is now 22. "We'd stand up and do cheers the entire game. I'd go to school the next day and my voice would be really hoarse."

At first, Adam, who is now a pharmacy supervisor for Kaiser Permanente, found it difficult to attend the weeknight matches, but in 2006 he finally bought season tickets – and he gave one of his seats to Jesse.

The other ticket went to Paul.

For years, Adam, Paul and Jesse have attended games together, three generations of Timbers fans enjoying their favorite pastime.

The group used to sit with the Timbers Army, but after Adam was involved in a motorcycle accident in 2009, it got a bit harder to keep up with the jumping and chanting.

When the Timbers entered MLS, Adam decided to buy season tickets in the Key Club section.

"I'm kind of a Timber Army retired," Adam says. "Although I always stand during the game. I got a seat especially so I would have a wall behind me."

Jesse went off to college at Boston University nearly four years ago and covered his dorm room with Timbers gear. He attends games when he returns home in

the summer. Paul stopped attending matches regularly in 2014 because the drive from Gresham became a bit too far for the 75-year-old. He still watches on TV.

But Adam doesn't miss a match.

He walks into the stadium two hours before each game and feels just as amped as he was as an 11-year-old, 40 years ago.

"It's something I haven't experienced with any other sport," Adam says. "There's just something magical about being in that park with that team." ∎

RIGHT: Portland Timbers coach Don Megson acknowledges the crowd at Civic Stadium after a season-ending loss to the Los Angeles Aztecs on Aug. 12, 1979. Brent Wojahn/The Oregonian/OregonLive

OPPOSITE: Players on the Portland Timbers and Seattle Sounders shake hands following the final whistle after the first game of the Portland Timbers' inaugural season on May 5, 1975. Brent Wojahn/The Oregonian/OregonLive

ABOVE: Peter Withe (#9) of the Portland Timbers competes for a ball in the air with Dave D'Errico (#2) of the Seattle Sounders during the first game of the Portland Timbers' inaugural season at Civic Stadium on May 5, 1975. Brent Wojahn/The Oregonian/OregonLive

RIGHT: Portland Commissioner Mildred Schwab cheers as Timbers players take a victory lap around the pitch at Civic Stadium after eliminating St. Louis from the North American Soccer League playoffs in 1975. Michael Lloyd/The Oregonian/OregonLive

FAR RIGHT: Barry Powell of the Portland Timbers races past a Sounders defender in the Timbers' first game at Civic Stadium as a member of the North American Soccer League, a 1-0 loss to Seattle on May 5, 1975. Brent Wojahn/The Oregonian/OregonLive

1976

Over 32,000 fans turn out on June 12 at what was then Civic Stadium to watch the Timbers play the New York Cosmos, who had the 36-year-old king of soccer Pele and star Italian striker Giorgio Chinaglia on their roster.

RIGHT: Giorgio Chinaglia warms up during a training session held at Catlin Gabel School before the Portland Timbers' home match against the New York Cosmos in 1976.

Donald Wilson/The Oregonian/OregonLive

1978

The Timbers make it to the NASL Conference Finals before losing to the Cosmos.

ABOVE: Fans line up outside Civic Stadium before tickets go on sale for the Portland Timbers' NASL playoff game against the Washington Diplomats.

Dale Swanson/The Oregonian/OregonLive

1975

LEFT: Barry Powell (#8) controls the ball on a rain-soaked pitch supported by teammate Tommy McLaren (#7) during the Portland Timbers' first game in their inaugural season, played on May 5, 1975 against the Seattle Sounders at Civic Stadium. Brent Wojahn/The Oregonian/OregonLive

BELOW: Elson Seale (left) of the Portland Timbers fights for possession during the 1978 season.

Claudia Howell/The Oregonian/OregonLive

1975

The North American Soccer League awards an expansion franchise to Portland. The Timbers would go 16-6 in their inaugural season and make it all the way to the NASL championship game – dubbed the Soccer Bowl – where they lost 2-0 to the Tampa Bay Rowdies.

BELOW: Local businessman James Horne meets the media and explains why he withdrew his bid to buy the Portland Timbers soccer club in 1982. Brent Wojahn/The Oregonian/OregonLive

1980

1982

The Timbers fold as a member of the NASL at the end of the 1982 season.

LEFT: Goalkeeper Bill Irwin was acquired by the Timbers in 1982. He returned to "Soccer City, USA" following his playing career and coached at the University of Portland for nearly 30 years.

The Oregonian/OregonLive

1989

The Timbers are resurrected under the ownership of local businessman Art Dixon as a member of the Western Soccer League. The team features University of Portland goalkeeper Kasey Keller.

LEFT: In 1989, Kasey Keller joined the Portland Timbers, where his stellar goalkeeping earned him Western Soccer League MVP honors.

The Oregonian/OregonLive

2001

The Timbers return to the field on May 11, 2001, as a United Soccer League franchise. A crowd of 12,295 fans watches from the stands of what was then called PGE Park as the Timbers beat the Seattle Sounders 2-0.

LEFT: Forward Mark Baena controls the ball during the Portland Timbers' home opener against the Seattle Sounders on May 11, 2001.

Robyn Larsen/The Oregonian/OregonLive

1990

LEFT: Midfielder John Bain of the Portland Timbers evades a defender during a game against the San Diego Nomads on April 20, 1990.

The Oregonian/OregonLive

1990

The Timbers fold for a second time after the 1990 season.

2005

For the first time in the Timbers' USL-era, an English Premier League team flies to Portland. A crowd of 15,376 fans, the largest attendance that the Timbers had attracted in five seasons, attends the July 23 match to watch the Timbers play to a scoreless draw with Sunderland AFC.

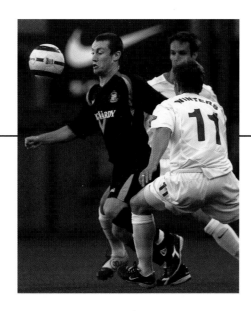

LEFT: Stephen Elliott of Sunderland dribbles past Brian Winters and Lee Morrison of the Portland Timbers in a game played at PGE Park.

Bruce Ely/The Oregonian/OregonLive

2005

2009

The Timbers are announced as Major League Soccer's 18th team on March 20 by Commissioner Don Garber.

RIGHT: Portland Timbers head coach Gavin Wilkinson juggles during practice at PGE Park on Aug. 21, 2009.

Steven Gibbons/The Oregonian/OregonLive

LEFT: Fans that make up the Timbers Army erupt in cheers as the Portland Timbers score their first goal against the rival Seattle Sounders in a game played at PGE Park on July 1, 2009. Thomas Boyd/The Oregonian/OregonLive

2009

The Timbers put together a 24-game unbeaten streak, one of the longest unbeaten streaks in U.S. soccer history.

2011

The Timbers play their first game as an MLS franchise on the road against the Colorado Rapids, losing 3-1.

LEFT: Portland Timbers forward Kenny Cooper fights for the ball in a game against the Colorado Rapids on March 19, 2011.

Thomas Boyd/The Oregonian/OregonLive

2010

ABOVE: Rodney Wallace (left) of the Portland Timbers celebrates with teammate Kalif Alhassan following Wallace's goal against the Chicago Fire on April 14, 2011.

Thomas Boyd/The Oregonian/OregonLive

LEFT: Fireworks light up the sky as fans in the Timbers Army unveil an elaborate tifo at Jeld-Wen Field before the Portland Timbers play the Chicago Fire on April 14, 2011.

Thomas Boyd/The Oregonian/OregonLive

2011

The Timbers beat the Chicago Fire 4-2 in their MLS home opener in front of 19,000 delirious, rain-drenched fans.

2012

The Timbers fire John Spencer and hire Caleb Porter as coach in the middle of the 2012 season. Porter takes over as coach after the season.

LEFT: Portland Timbers head coach John Spencer walks off the pitch following a loss to Spanish soccer club Valencia CF in a friendly played at Jeld-Wen Field on May 23, 2012.

Thomas Boyd/The Oregonian/OregonLive

2015

The Timbers are crowned Western Conference champions and a week later win the MLS Cup — both firsts.

2012

LEFT: Midfielder Will Johnson fights back tears as he and other Timbers players take a lap around the field, thanking fans after a loss to Real Salt Lake in the MLS Cup Playoffs on Nov. 24, 2013.

Motoya Nakamura/The Oregonian/OregonLive

RIGHT: Midfielder Diego Valeri waves to the Timbers Army following a loss to Real Salt Lake in the MLS Cup Playoffs at Jeld-Wen Field on Nov. 24, 2013.

Thomas Boyd/The Oregonian/OregonLive

2013

The Timbers make the MLS playoffs for the first time, advancing to the Western Conference Finals.

SEASON REWIND

ABOVE: Jorge Villafana draws contact from defender Jamison Olave as the Portland Timbers face Real Salt Lake in a game played at Providence Park on March 7. Thomas Boyd/The Oregonian/OregonLive

OPPOSITE: Timbers coach Caleb Porter watches from the sidelines as Portland faces Real Salt Lake at Providence Park on March 7. Thomas Boyd/The Oregonian/OregonLive

Timbers get off to slow start in early play

By Jamie Goldberg

MAY 16, 2015

The Portland Timbers arrived at preseason training camp in late January determined to learn from a disappointing 2014 season.

The club had missed the playoffs by just one point after a devastatingly slow start to the season. The team managed just five points in eight games before starting to turn things around.

"It was a wake up call," Timbers coach Caleb Porter said.

If they hoped to avoid another slow start, the Timbers would have to overcome some serious adversity early in 2015 as they tried to earn results without playmaker Diego Valeri and captain Will Johnson. Valeri was recovering from a torn ACL that he sustained on the last day of the 2014 season and Johnson was working his way back from a broken leg.

But despite the injuries and the letdown of 2014, Porter and his staff believed they had a strong core of players.

"In looking at the health of the club, we knew there weren't major things we needed to overhaul," Porter said before the season. "I knew we needed a couple pieces. We needed a few little adjustments, but we had a really good team."

The Timbers made the offseason decision to keep the majority of their team intact, bringing in just two new immediate starters in Nat Borchers and Adam Kwarasey to help shore up a defensive group that had

struggled in 2014.

From the first game of the season, it was clear that the Timbers had improved. They were putting in good performances and going toe-to-toe with some of the top teams in the league.

But the good performances weren't adding up to results.

The Timbers opened the year with a scoreless draw at home against Real Salt Lake where they took an impressive 18 shots, but couldn't find the back of the net. A week later, the Timbers pulled ahead of the LA Galaxy in stoppage time at Providence Park, but

then immediately gave up a goal to the Galaxy's Alan Gordon to settle for a 2-2 tie.

Two games later, Portland's back line gave up a late goal after an unusual mistake in stoppage time to lose 2-1 on the road to the Vancouver Whitecaps.

"There are some games this year, we should have won," Porter said. "We were playing very well and not winning."

While Portland's start didn't feel nearly as slow as it had in 2014, it was clear that there were reasons to be concerned.

After 12 games, Portland found itself sitting dead

last in the Western Conference standings with just 13 points – the same point total that they had accumulated after as many games when they missed playoffs in both 2012 and 2014.

This wasn't how the Timbers had expected their season to start, but they still had time to turn things around.

"Early on in the season, you know we had a few key guys out, some injuries, but we still felt like we were playing really good soccer," Timbers midfielder Jack Jewsbury said. "The results weren't coming, but we just stuck with our approach. We knew we had the ability and the belief in that locker room." ∎

ABOVE RIGHT: Midfielder Jack Jewsbury (left) celebrates his stoppage time goal with teammate Will Johnson (#4) as the Portland Timbers escaped with a 1-0 win over the San Jose Earthquakes at Providence Park on July 5. Randy L. Rasmussen/The Oregonian/OregonLive

ABOVE LEFT: Forward Gaston Fernandez celebrates a goal prematurely after an offside call erased the scoring play, but the Portland Timbers held on to beat the San Jose Earthquakes 1-0 at Providence Park on July 5. Randy L. Rasmussen/The Oregonian/OregonLive

LEFT: Portland Timbers players swarm midfielder Darlington Nagbe after he scored a first-half goal against the rival Seattle Sounders at Providence Park on June 28. Randy L. Rasmussen/The Oregonian/OregonLive

OPPOSITE: Midfielder Dairon Asprilla reacts after being hit in the jaw during the first half of a Portland Timbers game against the San Jose Earthquakes on July 5. Randy L. Rasmussen/The Oregonian/OregonLive

ABOVE: Midfielder Diego Valeri (right) hugs Fanendo Adi in front of the Providence Park crowd following a goal Valeri scored against the Vancouver Whitecaps on July 1. Thomas Boyd/The Oregonian/OregonLive

RIGHT: Portland Timbers goalkeeper Adam Kwarasey tries to stop a penalty kick attempt against Orlando City SC on April 12. Thomas Boyd/The Oregonian/OregonLive

OPPOSITE: LA Galaxy goalkeeper Brian Rowe snatches a ball sent in front of the goal before Portland Timbers defender Nat Borchers can get to it during a game on March 15. Thomas Boyd/The Oregonian/OregonLive

Fans send sharp message to Timbers

By Molly Blue

MAY 28, 2015

The Portland Timbers came into their May 27th matchup with DC United in dire need of a win. They entered the game tied for last place in the Western Conference standings after back-to-back losses. The offense was struggling to score and the defense hadn't been able to withstand the pressure to play a perfect match, game in and game out.

Fans, never shy to show their love for the Timbers, sprinkled some discontent around Providence Park in the form of banners.

One, a play on a British World War II slogan, read "Keep Calm All We Really Want Are Goals."

The Timbers Army unfurled a larger banner with the words "Same As It Ever Was" beneath a red line behind a goal.

The banner remained on the stand throughout the match and the Timbers gave the fans an inspired performance in a 1-0 win over DC United. Maximiliano Urruti scored in the fifth minute, and Portland threatened to boost the margin of victory even through four minutes of extra time.

After, Timbers coach Caleb Porter and midfielder Will Johnson, whose return to the pitch after rehabilitating a broken leg was celebrated by fans and the team alike, talked about how the Timbers appreciate the fans and don't want to let them down.

"Obviously, it has not been good enough," Johnson said. "Nobody in this locker room has ever put their hand up and said that where we are right now is good enough. We know where it is and (the fans) deserve better. We're trying to give it to them." ∎

LEFT: Timbers fans at Providence Park swing their scarves during a performance of the National Anthem before the Portland Timbers' game against DC United on May 27. Thomas Boyd/The Oregonian/OregonLive

OPPOSITE: Maximiliano Urruti gets to the ball before DC United defender Steven Birnbaum during a game played at Providence Park on May 27. Thomas Boyd/The Oregonian/OregonLive

ABOVE: Maximiliano Urruti scores the game's lone goal in the Timbers' 1-0 victory over DC United at Providence Park on May 27.

Thomas Boyd/The Oregonian/OregonLive

OPPOSITE: Winger Rodney Wallace attempts a shot against DC United on May 27. Thomas Boyd/The Oregonian/OregonLive

RIGHT: Winger Rodney Wallace stretches to keep the ball in play during a game against DC United at Providence Park on May 27.

Thomas Boyd/The Oregonian/OregonLive

OPPOSITE: Forward Maximiliano Urruti attempts to keep the ball away from a defender during a game against DC United on May 27.

Thomas Boyd/The Oregonian/OregonLive

Timbers acquire speedster Lucas Melano

By Jamie Goldberg

JULY 20, 2015

Three days after arriving in Portland this past summer, Lucas Melano sprinted up and down the field at Timbers training, dribbling around defenders and sending passes into the box with confidence.

Though it took time for Melano to adjust to Portland and his new club, the Argentine forward said he was ready to contribute from the start.

"Physically and sportingly I'm ready to play," said Melano at the time, through an interpreter. "I was training in Argentina. I'm excited to play, I'm ready to play."

The Timbers officially announced that they had signed Melano to a designated player contract on July 17 after rumors circulated for weeks that the 22-year-old would be joining the Timbers.

While the Timbers see Melano as a player that can develop into a top starter in the years to come, they also see the forward as a talented and speedy piece that can be an asset to the Timbers now.

"We need to look at his fitness," Porter said at the time. "He did get a full preseason, but he hasn't played a game in quite a while. We will bring him along in the right way, but we won't wait too long either."

Melano does not yet speak English and it was clear from training that it could take a little bit of time for the forward to start to understand his English-speaking teammates and coaches.

But Melano said the adjustment to Portland would be little bit easier because he was joining four other Argentine players on the Timbers' roster.

He said the other Argentines have translated instructions for him on the field and have helped him adjust.

"It has been really helpful," said Melano at the time, through an interpreter. "They've been helping me a lot so far."

Timbers midfielder Diego Valeri, who was the first Argentine player to join the Timbers in 2013, also tried to make Melano feel welcomed.

During Melano's first weekend in Portland, Valeri picked him up at his hotel and took him on a tour of

ABOVE: Forward Lucas Melano speeds past defenders on a run at goal during the first leg of the Portland Timbers' Western Conference Championship match against FC Dallas in the MLS Cup Playoffs on Nov. 22. Thomas Boyd/The Oregonian/OregonLive

OPPOSITE: Lucas Melano heads the ball toward his teammates in a game against the New York Red Bulls on Sept. 20. Thomas Boyd/The Oregonian/OregonLive

the city. The two players then went back to Valeri's home in Northwest Portland to talk about the Timbers, Portland as a city and Major League Soccer.

"Everybody needs that," Valeri said. "I know it's very important the first days when you are far (away) from your country to be close to someone who (can) help you. ... We are in rhythm now. He has a couple months to adapt quickly."

The Timbers first reached out to Melano in June to discuss the possible transfer to Portland.

Melano said he was excited at the prospect of playing in the MLS with a team that already had a large contingent of Argentine players. He said he jumped at the opportunity to come to Portland.

"I'm very happy to be here," said Melano, through an interpreter.

Porter said that Melano's athleticism really stood out to the Timbers when they decided to bring him to Portland.

"He's a guy that will hopefully eliminate defenders, individually at times, through his movement, running behind, and off the dribble," Porter said. "He's a guy that if he's behind the back four, you're not catching him." ∎

ABOVE RIGHT: Timbers forward Lucas Melano fires a shot on goal in a game against the Chicago Fire on Aug. 7.
Thomas Boyd/The Oregonian/OregonLive

RIGHT: Lucas Melano celebrates his late goal that secured a Timbers victory over FC Dallas during the second leg of the Western Conference Championship at Toyota Stadium in Frisco, Texas, on Nov. 29. Stewart F. House/The Oregonian/OregonLive

LUCAS MELANO

Age: 22
Height: 6'1"
Position: Forward
Birthplace: Hernando, Argentina
Lucas Melano Trivia: Melano played in Argentina for Lanus, the same club Diego Valeri played for.

2015 Stats
Regular-Season Goals: 1
Regular-Season Assists: 3
Postseason Goals: 1
Postseason Assists: 1

Diego Valeri attempts to work way back from two injuries

By Jamie Goldberg

AUG. 7, 2015

After a grueling six months slowly rehabbing from a torn ACL, Diego Valeri finally jogged out onto the field to a deafening cheer from the crowd at Providence Park 52 minutes into a game against the Vancouver Whitecaps on May 2.

It felt like a momentous occasion for the Portland Timbers, who had desperately missed their best player during the first two months of the season.

But Valeri's return was short-lived.

Just three weeks after his season debut, the 29-year-old Argentine midfielder sprained his ankle early in a match at Toronto FC. It took a month before he made another appearance.

"Always when you get an injury, it's hard," Valeri said. "It's hard to rehab, it's hard when you get back to the field."

Valeri returned to the starting lineup, but the playmaker struggled to reach top form.

Valeri, who led Portland in both goals and assists in 2013 and 2014, recording 21 goals and 27 assists over the two seasons, scored two goals and recorded eight assists during the regular season.

The Timbers missed a healthy Valeri.

"Any player in his situation is going to be coming along still," Timbers coach Caleb Porter said. "Obviously, he was out six and a half months with an ACL and then he's back a couple games and then he's out with an

ankle for three, four games, so it's been stop, start."

Timbers captain Will Johnson, who broke his leg last September, rehabbed alongside Valeri during the offseason and the early months of the 2015 season.

Johnson said even after a player recovers from an injury, it still takes time for his body to readjust to the stress of playing full 90-minute games.

"It just takes a lot of time," Johnson said. "Your body is still healing."

Getting Valeri to redevelop a strong chemistry with the rest of the players in the attack also proved difficult, given the inconsistency of the lineup for much of the season.

While Valeri recovered from his injuries, the rest

of Portland's attacking players had been unable to consistently pick up the slack.

But while the Timbers expect production from

ABOVE: Midfielders Diego Valeri (left) and Will Johnson rehab on the sidelines during the opening of preseason training for the Portland Timbers at Providence Park on Jan. 23. Kristyna Wentz-Graff/The Oregonian/OregonLive

OPPOSITE: Portland Timbers midfielder Diego Valeri explodes with emotion after scoring a goal against the Vancouver Whitecaps on July 18. Thomas Boyd/The Oregonian/OregonLive

Steve Clark 27 seconds into the match to score on a sliding shot as the Timbers went on to win 2-1.

After a year of struggles, Valeri was named MLS Cup MVP for his performance and had the opportunity to raise the MLS Cup high.

"For me, it was a long, long year," Valeri said. "I worked hard. I knew that I could get back. I knew that this could happen." ■

LEFT: Diego Valeri fights for possession of the ball against San Jose Earthquakes defender Victor Bernardez during the Portland Timbers' 1-0 win on July 5. Randy L. Rasmussen/The Oregonian/OregonLive

OPPOSITE: Portland Timbers owner Merritt Paulson (right) congratulates Diego Valeri after a 4-1 victory over the rival Seattle Sounders on June 28. Randy L. Rasmussen/The Oregonian/OregonLive

DIEGO VALERI

Age: 29
Height: 5'10"
Position: Midfielder
Birthplace: Valentin Alsina, Argentina
Diego Valeri Trivia: In 2013 he led MLS with 13 assists.

2015 Stats
Regular-Season Goals: 2
Regular-Season Assists: 8
Postseason Goals: 1
Postseason Assists: 4

multiple players, no player is more vital to Portland's attack than Valeri.

As the Timbers headed into the final stretch of the regular season, locked in a tight Western Conference playoff race, they hoped that Valeri would once again return to top form and lead the attack.

"We need our top guys to produce and score goals," Porter said. "I'm confident he will because he's done that every year and he's a very good player."

There were signs late in the season that Valeri was starting to return to full strength. The Argentine playmaker picked up five assists in the final nine games of the season.

But it was in the playoffs, with everything on the line, that Valeri really came to life on the field.

He recorded an assist on Rodney Wallace's opening goal against Sporting Kansas City and showed amazing chemistry with his teammates in the conference semifinals against the Vancouver Whitecaps, recording the game-winning assist on Fanendo Adi's goal in the second leg of the series. Valeri recorded two more assists against FC Dallas in the second leg of the Western Conference Championship series.

Then, in the MLS Cup Final, Valeri wasted no time.

He scored the fastest goal in MLS Cup history, taking advantage of a poor touch by Columbus goalkeeper

New formation brings out best in Darlington Nagbe

By Jamie Goldberg

NOV. 5, 2015

Everything changed for the Portland Timbers on Oct. 3.

After a disheartening 1-0 home loss that left the Timbers below the red line with just three games to play, Caleb Porter and his staff decided that they needed to alter their formation.

Porter specifically hoped that the new offensive-minded formation would bring out the best in Darlington Nagbe.

"We were getting chances and we were playing well, but something was missing," Porter said. "With Darlington, you look at him and he wasn't contributing as much as we felt he could."

The Timbers unveiled their new formation at Real Salt Lake on Oct. 14, setting up in an offensive-heavy 4-3-3 with a lone defensive midfielder. The change allowed Nagbe to move into a central role and play more as box-to-box midfielder.

It paid off.

The new formation gave Nagbe the flexibility to float around the field and gave the Timbers a creative presence in the center of the park. Nagbe recorded three goals and an assist in the final two games of the regular season.

"(The formation change) was good," Nagbe said. "I feel like the team felt good in it...Attacking-wise it was natural. I could get on the ball a little bit more."

Nagbe continued to be a dominant central force during the playoffs. In the first leg of the Western Conference semifinals against the Vancouver Whitecaps, Porter had Nagbe play a bit deeper on the field and encouraged the talented midfielder to control the center of the pitch.

The 25-year-old finished the game with 104 touches — way more than anyone else on the field — 77 passes, an 89.6 percent passing accuracy, eight successful dribbles, nine recoveries and three tackles won.

"The biggest reason he's impacted the game more is he's just more free to float wherever he wants to, to find the game, to get on the ball," Porter said then. "You saw that (against Vancouver). He was the most involved player on the field."

At the time, Porter said he liked the way that Nagbe and Timbers playmaker Diego Valeri complemented each other in the new formation. With Nagbe dropping deeper in the center of the park, Valeri has had the freedom to player higher and float around the pitch in the attack.

"If you play with Darlington and me in the middle, you will try to attack more and be more on the ball," Valeri said. "We are trying to do that...We have to read

ABOVE: Portland Timbers midfielder Darlington Nagbe is pulled off the ball during a run in the first half of a game against the Colorado Rapids on Oct. 25. Randy L. Rasmussen/The Oregonian/OregonLive

OPPOSITE: Forward Fanendo Adi heads a ball into the box during the Portland Timbers' 4-1 win over the Colorado Rapids at Providence Park on Oct. 25. Randy L. Rasmussen/The Oregonian/OregonLive

ABOVE: Midfielder Darlington Nagbe tries to work the ball into scoring position as heavy rain falls on the pitch during a Portland Timbers victory over the Colorado Rapids on Oct. 25.
Randy L. Rasmussen/The Oregonian/OregonLive

OPPOSITE: Darlington Nagbe tries to maneuver past Colorado Rapids midfielder Lucas Pittinari in a game at Providence Park on Oct. 25. Randy L. Rasmussen/The Oregonian/OregonLive

each other well and occupy some defensive spots when we lose the ball."

While Porter knew that the new formation would provide an offensive spark, he was initially worried that the club's defense might suffer.

But the attacking players – led by Nagbe – embraced their defensive responsibilities.

When the Timbers lost possession, Nagbe did a good job to drop back and connect with Portland's lone holding midfielder, which allowed the Timbers to almost revert to a double-pivot system on defense, while still having the advantage of an extra player in the attack.

"(Nagbe's) not a tenacious ball winner, but because he's so athletic, he picks up a lot of loose balls that fall in the midfield and he's able to gobble up space," Porter said. "Funny enough, he ends up defending really well and he does it more through his athleticism and positioning. We didn't know if he was going to be able to defensively switch gears and figure out where to be, but he's done extremely well both sides of the ball." ∎

DARLINGTON NAGBE

Age: 25
Height: 5'9"
Position: Midfielder/Forward
Birthplace: Monrovia, Liberia
Darlington Nagbe Trivia: His father, Joe, is a former captain of the Liberian National Team.

2015 Stats
Regular-Season Goals: 5
Regular-Season Assists: 5
Postseason Goals: 0
Postseason Assists: 2

ABOVE LEFT: Darlington Nagbe holds his 23-month-old daughter, Mila, as fans welcome the Timbers back to Portland on Nov. 30, following the team's victory over FC Dallas in the Western Conference Championship. Stephanie Yao Long/The Oregonian/OregonLive

LEFT: Portland Timbers midfielder Darlington Nagbe assists volunteers in home construction with Habitat for Humanity in Beaverton on June 11. Bruce Ely/The Oregonian/OregonLive

OPPOSITE: Darlington Nagbe splits defenders on a run at goal during the Portland Timbers' game against the New England Revolution on June 6. Thomas Boyd/The Oregonian/OregonLive

LEFT: Darlington Nagbe turns away from a defender in the Portland Timbers' 1-0 win over the San Jose Earthquakes on July 5. Randy L. Rasmussen/The Oregonian/OregonLive

OPPOSITE: Seattle defender Oniel Fisher tries to pull Darlington Nagbe (front) off the ball during the Portland Timbers' 4-1 win over the Seattle Sounders on June 28. Randy L. Rasmussen/The Oregonian/OregonLive

ABOVE: Darlington Nagbe beats Orlando City FC midfielder Kevin Molino to the ball for a header in a game played at Providence Park on April 12. Thomas Boyd/The Oregonian/OregonLive

OPPOSITE: Darlington Nagbe heads the ball to himself to keep a run on goal alive during a game against the New York Red Bulls on Sept. 20. Thomas Boyd/The Oregonian/OregonLive

THE PLAYOFFS

ABOVE: Liam Ridgewell reacts after his penalty kick against Sporting Kansas City at Providence Park, Oct. 29. After the season, Ridgewell was named the Timbers Defender of the Year. Randy L. Rasmussen/The Oregonian/OregonLive

OPPOSITE: Sporting Kansas City goalkeeper Jon Kempin walks toward the penalty spot to take his turn after Adam Kwarasey converted his penalty kick a few seconds earlier. Kempin's miss gave the Timbers a 7-6 win on penalty kicks after the teams were tied 2-2 after 120 minutes of regulation time at Providence Park on Oct. 29.

Randy L. Rasmussen/The Oregonian/OregonLive

Knockout Round: Timbers triumph in epic shootout

By Jamie Goldberg

OCT. 29, 2015

Even after big games, Portland Timbers coach Caleb Porter tries not to show much emotion. He tends to keep the highs low and the lows high and is always focused on the next task at hand.

But even Porter couldn't hide his excitement after this win.

He strutted into the media conference room after the game with a huge smile on his face and yelled out, "How about that!"

The Timbers beat Sporting Kansas City 7-6 on penalty kicks in an epic knockout game on Oct. 29 after the two clubs played to a 2-2 draw over 120 minutes of regulation in front of 21,144 fans at Providence Park.

"It's a game of moments and a game of inches and we found those plays and we won those moments," Porter said after the game. "That's why we're moving on."

In a wild and dramatic finish to an already exciting game, the Timbers and Sporting Kansas City combined for a total 22 penalty kicks. Kansas City had a chance to win it on its ninth penalty kick, but Saad Abdul-Salaam's attempt somehow hit off both posts before bouncing out to keep the Timbers alive.

"Something kept that ball out," Porter said. "I don't know what it was. Maybe it was the air from (the Timbers Army) yelling so much. ... I'm going to credit the Timbers Army for keeping that last ball out."

Timbers goalkeeper Adam Kwarasey converted Portland's last penalty kick, before stopping one final attempt from Sporting Kansas City goalkeeper Jon Kempin to give the Timbers the victory.

As Kwarasey made the diving stop, Portland's bench cleared and players raced to embrace Kwarasey in a massive hug.

"It was like a movie," Kwarasey said.

The Timbers entered the game well-prepared for the pressure of the MLS Cup Playoffs.

After falling below the red line in early October, Portland played its final three games of the regular season with its backs against the wall, managing to score a whopping 10 goals en route to three victories to finish third in the Western Conference standings.

And the Timbers had to perform under immense pressure once again.

Rodney Wallace gave the Timbers the lead in the 57th minute, when he sent a sliding, left-footed shot from close range into the back of the net. But Sporting Kansas City fought back with a header from Kevin Ellis in the 87th minute to take the game into extra time.

Kansas City quickly took control in extra time as forward Krisztian Nemeth beat midfielder George Fochive in the box and fired a shot from a tough angle into the back of the net in the 96th minute to give SKC the 2-1 lead.

The Timbers could have easily caved under the pressure, but instead they kept fighting.

Maximiliano Urruti, who came on for Fanendo Adi ahead of the second period of extra time, scored the equalizer off a beautiful cross from Dairon Asprilla in the 118th minute to give Portland new life.

"This season, this is what we've been about," Timbers defender Liam Ridgewell said after the game. "Playing all the way until the end, coming from behind, doing something when people have written us off." ∎

ABOVE: Maximiliano Urruti reacts after converting his penalty kick against Sporting Kansas City. Randy L. Rasmussen/The Oregonian/OregonLive

ABOVE LEFT: Timbers goalkeeper Adam Kwarasey was the 11th player to shoot for the Timbers during the penalty kick phase. He converted his kick, then stopped the attempt by Sporting Kansas City goalkeeper Jon Kempin to seal the win for Portland. Randy L. Rasmussen/The Oregonian/OregonLive

LEFT: Timbers players wait and hope as the penalty kick phase remains deadlocked. Randy L. Rasmussen/The Oregonian/OregonLive

OPPOSITE: Maximiliano Urruti celebrates his tying goal in the 118th minute. Randy L. Rasmussen/The Oregonian/OregonLive

ABOVE: Timbers fans celebrate the win after Portland prevails 7-6 on penalty kicks. Randy L. Rasmussen/The Oregonian/OregonLive

OPPOSITE: Timbers players rejoice as Sporting Kansas City goalkeeper Jon Kempin walks off the pitch after his penalty kick attempt was saved by Adam Kwarasey. Randy L. Rasmussen/The Oregonian/OregonLive

Western Conference Semifinals: Timbers oust Cascadia rivals Vancouver

By Jamie Goldberg

NOV. 8, 2015

VANCOUVER, British Columbia — The Portland Timbers failed to earn a single win in their first four meetings with the Vancouver Whitecaps in 2015.

But the Timbers came through when it counted most.

The Timbers advanced to the Western Conference finals after beating the Whitecaps 2-0 on Nov. 8 in the second leg of the conference semifinals in front of 27,837 fans at BC Place. The two clubs entered the match tied on aggregate-score in the two-leg series after playing to a scoreless draw at Providence Park on Nov. 1.

Portland knew that an early goal would put the club in a great position to advance to the conference finals to face Dallas.

Due to the away goal rule, Portland needed to earn only a draw that included at least one goal to advance. Under the rule, the team that scores more away goals moves on if the aggregate-score remains tied at the end of a two-leg series.

The Timbers had a lot of difficulty scoring goals in the first half during the season. Just 10 of Portland's 41 regular season goals came in the first 45 minutes of games in 2015.

But both the Timbers and Whitecaps came out looking to score early, and it was Portland that managed to

find the opening goal.

"We went for the first goal and we got it," Timbers coach Caleb Porter said after the game. "I thought it was very well-managed overall."

Timbers midfielder Diego Valeri got on the end of a pass from Rodney Wallace in the 31st minute and made a beautiful run toward the byline before cutting the ball back to Adi in the center of the box. Adi fired a shot into the top of the net to put the Timbers up 1-0.

"We are very confident," Adi said after the game. "You

ABOVE: Timber Joey hoists a slice of log for goalkeeper Adam Kwarasey after Kwarasey held the Vancouver Whitecaps scoreless in the opening match of the Western Conference Semifinals on Nov. 1, at Providence Park. Thomas Boyd/The Oregonian/OregonLive

OPPOSITE: Darlington Nagbe played 90 minutes, took two shots, and was fouled once during the opening match at Providence Park.

Thomas Boyd/The Oregonian/OregonLive

can't be more confident than we are at the moment."

The Whitecaps never recovered.

Though Vancouver continued to pressure the Timbers, they were unable to really challenge Timbers goalkeeper Adam Kwarasey or mount any sort of comeback. Whitecaps midfielder Kekuta Manneh left the game in the 26th minute with an injury, which seriously hurt Vancouver's chances in the game as well.

"Defensively, we were outstanding," Porter said when it was over. "They had a hard time creating much."

Timbers midfielder Diego Chara put the icing on the cake with a goal in stoppage time to give the Timbers the 2-0 lead.

Still, Portland didn't leave the game unscathed.

Valeri and Wallace both picked up yellow cards in the second half and would be suspended for the first leg of the Western Conference finals vs. Dallas on Nov. 22 because of yellow card accumulation.

Due to the suspensions, the Timbers would definitely be short-handed when they hosted Dallas in the first leg of the conference finals.

But the surging Timbers remained unfazed.

"I think we're still scratching the surface of the level this team can play at," Porter said. "This team has a lot of belief that we can win it all this year." ∎

OPPOSITE: Rodney Wallace committed three fouls during the opening match of semifinal play at Providence Park.

Thomas Boyd/The Oregonian/OregonLive

RIGHT: Fanendo Adi had only one shot on goal during his 71 minutes played Nov. 1 at Providence Park. He also committed two fouls before being replaced by Maximiliano Urruti. Thomas Boyd/The Oregonian/OregonLive

OPPOSITE: Caleb Porter managed his team to a scoreless draw in the first round of the Western Conference Semifinals on Nov. 1, at Providence Park.

Thomas Boyd/The Oregonian/OregonLive

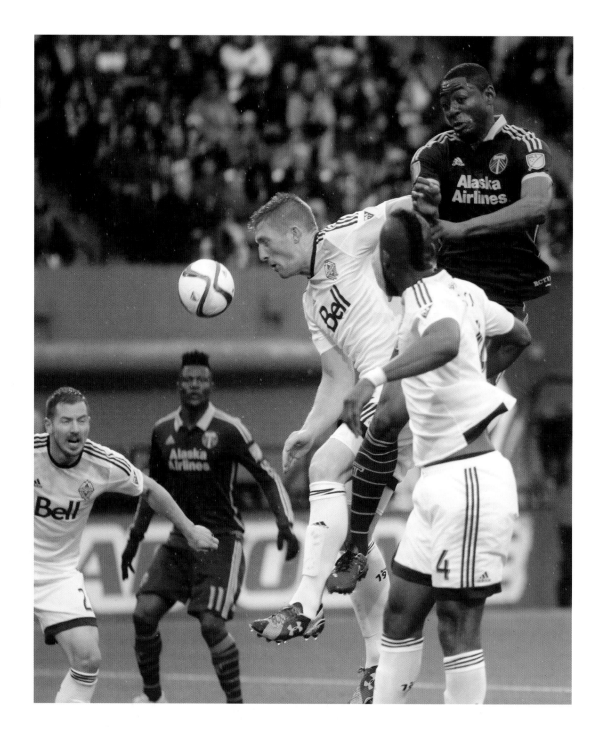

Western Conference Finals: Timbers hold off Dallas to advance

By Jamie Goldberg

NOV. 29, 2015

FRISCO, Texas — In 1975, the Portland Timbers captured the attention of the Rose City as they made a run all the way to the title game of the North American Soccer League in their inaugural season as a franchise before falling to the Tampa Bay Rowdies.

Forty years later, the Timbers finally found themselves back in the title game after winning the Western Conference Championship.

The Timbers played to a 2-2 draw against FC Dallas on Nov. 29 in front of 20,966 fans at Toyota Stadium. The tie sent the Timbers to the MLS Cup Final for the first time in club history with a 5-3 aggregate-score win. The victory also marked the first time in MLS history that a Cascadia team had won a Western Conference title.

ABOVE RIGHT: Dairon Asprilla played 90 minutes and scored the second of Portland's three goals in the opening match of the Western Conference Championships against FC Dallas at Providence Park on Nov. 22. He also had an assist on Liam Ridgewell's opening score.

Thomas Boyd/The Oregonian/OregonLive

OPPOSITE: Nat Borchers celebrates with teammates after scoring the Timbers' final goal, in stoppage time, at Providence Park.

Thomas Boyd/The Oregonian/OregonLive

"This is a great moment for this club," Timbers coach Caleb Porter said after the game. "This is our first trophy, but we want the biggest trophy and we have one more game still to achieve that."

Portland entered the match up 3-1 in the series after beating Dallas at home, which enabled the Timbers to advance to the MLS Cup Final with the draw.

"I think for us to be able to give back to our fans that have stuck with us through thick and thin makes it all the more special," Timbers midfielder Jack Jewsbury said after the game. "We have one more step to go to really feel good about the season."

Even though Portland entered the late November match against Dallas with a critical two-goal cushion, Porter didn't want his team just to sit back and try to protect the lead all game. Instead, he started an offense-heavy formation and the Timbers took an aggressive approach to the match.

The approach was effective for much of the game as the Timbers held Dallas scoreless in the first half, while still managing to put pressure on the Texas side in the attack.

The Timbers finally broke through in the 54th minute when Diego Valeri cut a ball back in the box to Fanendo Adi, who turned and fired a shot into the back of the net, giving Portland a 1-0 lead in the game and what felt like an insurmountable 4-1 aggregate-score lead in the series.

But the Timbers let down their guard just enough and Dallas fought back.

Dallas defender Ryan Hollingshead drilled in a pass from Mauro Diaz in the 68th minute to close the gap. Dallas striker Blas Perez then headed-home a free kick from Diaz in the 73rd minute to give Dallas a 2-1 lead in the game and pull within one goal of the Timbers in aggregate-score.

Dallas continued to pressure Portland late in the game as it looked for the series equalizer. Perez nearly scored in stoppage time, but Timbers defender Nat Borchers made an incredible block in the box to allow Portland to hold on to the lead.

"(Borchers) makes that big stop and to be honest that changes the whole series," Jewsbury said after the game. "He's been great for us all year and I'm just excited to have him as a part of this team."

The Timbers finally put the game out of reach late in stoppage time when Valeri sent a back-heel pass in the box to Lucas Melano, who dribbled around the Dallas defense and sent the ball into the net.

"They put pressure on us," Valeri said. "They played really well I think in the second half, but we knew that we could score on the counter (attack) and we did it."

Less than two months earlier, the Timbers were simply fighting to earn a spot in the playoffs. The possibility of earning a spot in the MLS Cup Final seemed unlikely.

But with their backs against the wall, the Timbers continued to believe that they could achieve something.

"I think sometimes it just felt like the only people that believed in our cause were us," Borchers said after the game. "I'm just really proud how we've responded to all that pressure. It's not easy."

After the game, the Timbers players raised the club's first MLS trophy above their heads, celebrating as the rain poured down on the field at Toyota Stadium.

The players recognized that it was a monumental moment in the franchise's 40-year history. But they still weren't satisfied.

"They have a belief, a true belief that we're going to win MLS Cup," Porter said. ∎

ABOVE: Liam Ridgewell scored the first goal of the game in the 23rd minute with assists from Dairon Asprilla and Darlington Nagbe.

Thomas Boyd/The Oregonian/OregonLive

OPPOSITE TOP AND BOTTOM RIGHT: Liam Ridgewell celebrates with teammates after scoring the opening goal of the match at Providence Park. Thomas Boyd/The Oregonian/OregonLive

OPPOSITE BOTTOM LEFT: Rodney Wallace gets a header over FC Dallas defender/midfielder Je-Vaughn Watson during the second match of the Western Conference Championships at Toyota Stadium in Frisco, Texas, on Nov. 29. Stewart F. House/The Oregonian/OregonLive

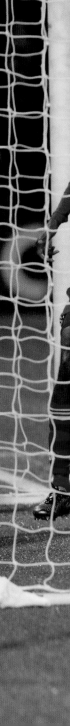

ABOVE LEFT: Darlington Nagbe battles for position with FC Dallas defender Matt Hedges as cold rain begins to fall during the second half of the Western Conference Championships at Toyota Stadium. Stewart F. House/The Oregonian/OregonLive

ABOVE RIGHT: Matt Hedges raises his hands after failing to keep Nat Borchers from scoring in stoppage time at Providence Park. Thomas Boyd/The Oregonian/OregonLive

RIGHT: Timbers fans who traveled to Texas were able to celebrate after a 2-2 tie propelled the Timbers to the MLS Cup final. Stewart F. House/The Oregonian/OregonLive

OPPOSITE: Nat Borchers' shot off a header by Norberto Paparatto clears the right post for the third goal of the opening match at Providence Park. Thomas Boyd/The Oregonian/OregonLive

ABOVE: Portland Timbers forward Lucas Melano confuses FC Dallas goalkeeper Jesse Gonzalez to score what would be the decisive goal late in the second half at Toyota Stadium in Frisco, Texas, on Nov. 29. Stewart F. House/The Oregonian/OregonLive

ABOVE RIGHT: FC Dallas midfielder Michael Barrios collides with Maximiliano Urruti at Toyota Stadium. Urruti replaced Fanendo Adi with five minutes remaining in the match. Stewart F. House/The Oregonian/OregonLive

RIGHT: Jenelle Premo (left) and Austin Putnam (center) made the trip from Portland to cheer with Timbers fans before the start of the game at Toyota Stadium. Stewart F. House/The Oregonian/OregonLive

OPPOSITE: The Timbers celebrate in Texas after a 2-2 tie against Dallas advanced the team to the MLS Cup final. Stewart F. House/The Oregonian/OregonLive

MLS Cup: Timbers came. They sawed. They conquered.

By Jamie Goldberg

DEC. 6, 2015

COLUMBUS, Ohio — The Portland Timbers jumped up and down at midfield, as thousands of Timbers fans looked on from the stands, waving flags and singing in a moment of pure elation.

It was a very long time before the players slowly made their way off the field, still holding the MLS Cup high.

Portland beat the Columbus Crew 2-1 at MAPFRE Stadium in Columbus in front of 21,747 fans on Dec. 6 to win its first MLS Cup in club history.

"I don't think it has sunk in yet that there's no next game," Timbers coach Caleb Porter said after the game. "We're raising the trophy and we're the best team in MLS this year."

The Timbers became the first men's professional team to win a league championship trophy for Portland since the Trail Blazers won the 1977 NBA Championship. The championship marked the Timbers' first league title in a 40-year history that spanned three different leagues.

For much of the year, it seemed improbable that the Timbers would be playing for the MLS Cup, let alone hoisting the coveted trophy as the last team standing.

"Every time people thought we were down and out, we'd pop up with a big result," Porter said after the game. "The players deserve credit for that. That shows their character. We knew if we could get hot and start scoring goals that we had a very strong mentality in this team."

The Timbers came together late in the year, closing out the regular season with three consecutive wins after a key formation change, before going unbeaten in an incredible playoff run that led them to the victory in Columbus.

Despite all the ups and downs of the season, the Timbers never stopped believing, and it showed on the field.

"We have a good locker room," Timbers defender Nat Borchers said after the game. "Everybody was with us throughout this run. It wasn't just the guys that started the game. It was the whole roster. That makes a big difference when you want to win a championship."

Like they had been for much of the playoffs, the Timbers entered the MLS Cup Final as the underdogs.

ABOVE LEFT: Lucas Melano hoists the trophy as confetti falls on the stage and Portland Timbers players celebrate after winning the MLS Cup at MAPFRE Stadium in Columbus, Ohio, on Dec. 6. Thomas Boyd/The Oregonian/OregonLive

OPPOSITE: Will Johnson (left) and Liam Ridgewell raise the trophy as fellow Timbers players celebrate on the pitch after winning the MLS Cup. Thomas Boyd/The Oregonian/OregonLive

Even Columbus players said before the game that they liked the matchup against the Timbers. Those comments only gave Portland more motivation.

"It was motivating because Columbus players, they were talking ahead of time," Timbers defender Jorge Villafana said. "I think your talk should be when you play, what you do on the field, and I think that's what kept us alive the whole season. We were humble. We never talked that we were the best team. We showed it on the field."

Portland didn't play like underdogs.

Timbers midfielder Diego Valeri took advantage of a heavy touch from Crew goalkeeper Steve Clark 27 seconds into the match and sent a sliding shot into the net to give Portland an early lead.

Valeri's goal was by far the fastest goal scored in MLS Cup history.

"I knew that this could happen," said Valeri, who was named MLS Cup MVP. "When you work hard, when you sacrifice, you can see it in every training and every game. ... I will keep this in my heart."

The Timbers doubled their lead in the seventh minute when Rodney Wallace dove and headed-home a cross from Lucas Melano. As Wallace and the rest of the Timbers ran to the corner flag to celebrate, Crew fans hurled cans onto the field, forcing the players to cut their celebration short as they tried to avoid getting hit.

"A lot of people probably, I think, felt that we were maybe satisfied winning the Western Conference,

---

RIGHT: Rodney Wallace fights for position during the first half of the MLS Cup final. Thomas Boyd/The Oregonian/OregonLive

OPPOSITE: Players watch the ball bounce on the goal line before being cleared during a tense moment in the game at the MLS Cup final. Randy L. Rasmussen/The Oregonian/OregonLive

holding that trophy," Timbers defender Jack Jewsbury said after the game. "But we wanted to come in here, a tough place to play with all their fans and everything on the line, and play a great game."

The Crew pulled a goal back in the 18th minute when Kei Kamara put a right-footed shot into the net from close-range after a series of defensive miscues from the Timbers.

Adam Kwarasey had a chance to catch an initial cross from Crew defender Harrison Afful, but couldn't get above Kamara. Timbers midfielder Diego Chara managed to get a touch on the ball as it bounced around the box but mistakenly tapped it to Kamara as he tried to clear it.

The game was sloppy and physical at times, but the Timbers held strong for the entire 90 minutes, relying on a complete team defensive effort to hold the Crew to just one shot on target.

"When we got rolling and we got confident, it was going to take something special to stop us," Jewsbury said.

When Porter took over as coach in 2013, he envisioned putting together a team that would one day be raising trophies.

The Timbers finished first in the Western Conference in 2013 but fell short as they lost to Real Salt Lake in the Western Conference Championship series. A year later, they missed the playoffs by just one point.

But the team kept plugging away.

"You always believe," Porter said. "You never win something like this unless you believe, unless you expect it." ■

ABOVE: Nat Borchers congratulates Rodney Wallace on his goal that gave the Portland Timbers a 2-0 lead over the Columbus Crew in the first half of the MLS Cup final. Thomas Boyd/The Oregonian/OregonLive

ABOVE RIGHT: Portland Timbers winger Rodney Wallace celebrates after scoring his team's second goal on a diving header in the seventh minute of the MLS Cup final.

Thomas Boyd/The Oregonian/OregonLive

RIGHT: Timbers players celebrate their first goal scored off a deflection in the first minute of the contest by Diego Valeri during the MLS Cup final.

Thomas Boyd/The Oregonian/OregonLive

ABOVE: Portland Timbers coach Caleb Porter looks on during the MLS Cup final between the Portland Timbers and the Columbus Crew on Dec. 6. Thomas Boyd/The Oregonian/OregonLive

LEFT: Goalkeeper Adam Kwarasey (center) clears the ball late in the game during the MLS Cup final between the Portland Timbers and the Columbus Crew. Randy L. Rasmussen/The Oregonian/OregonLive

ABOVE: Timber Joey poses in front of the Portland Timbers' victory log outside Providence Park after it was loaded on a Western Star 4900 truck to be transported to Columbus, Ohio, for the MLS Cup final. Kristyna Wentz-Graff/The Oregonian/OregonLive

ABOVE RIGHT: Timbers fans at MAPFRE Stadium in Columbus, Ohio, erupt in cheers at the final whistle of the MLS Cup final on Dec. 6.

Randy L. Rasmussen/The Oregonian/OregonLive

RIGHT: Coach Caleb Porter points to the Timbers Army and Portland fans in the crowd who remained for postgame celebrations at MAPFRE Stadium after his team captured the MLS Cup.

Thomas Boyd/The Oregonian/OregonLive

OPPOSITE: Nat Borchers celebrates with the MLS Cup following the Portland Timbers victory over the Columbus Crew at MAPFRE Stadium.

Randy L. Rasmussen/The Oregonian/OregonLive

ABOVE: Liam Ridgewell kisses the MLS Cup as players leave the pitch following the Portland Timbers' 2-1 win over the Columbus Crew on Dec. 6.

Randy L. Rasmussen/The Oregonian/OregonLive

OPPOSITE: As confetti falls, Timbers players celebrate on the pitch after winning the MLS Cup at MAPFRE Stadium in Columbus, Ohio, on Dec. 6.

Thomas Boyd/The Oregonian/OregonLive

RIGHT: Defender Liam Ridgewell raises the MLS Cup during postgame celebrations in the locker room following the Portland Timbers' 2-1 win over the Columbus Crew on Dec. 6. Thomas Boyd/The Oregonian/OregonLive

BELOW RIGHT: Liam Ridgewell hoists the trophy as champagne spray fills the locker room and Portland Timbers players celebrate after winning the MLS Cup in Columbus, Ohio.
Thomas Boyd/The Oregonian/OregonLive

OPPOSITE: Champagne-soaked Portland Timbers players pose for a photo in the locker room after winning the MLS Cup over Columbus Crew SC at MAPFRE Stadium in Columbus, Ohio.
Thomas Boyd/The Oregonian/OregonLive

Cup victory shows that transformation of Timbers is complete

By John Canzano

DEC. 6, 2015

The championship match ended. A title drought ended. Amid Caleb Porter's tears and Merritt Paulson's hugs, something entirely else began.

A city jumped onto the back of an MLS franchise. Portland beat Columbus 2-1.

If you were surprised, you haven't been paying attention. If you weren't delighted, you aren't alive. Because this soccer club transformed itself this season, remarkably, from a team that couldn't win into a rising tide that wasn't going to be held back.

In the run up to the championship match, Porter made a confession: "I know we're going to win it. I can feel it. Sometimes you just know it in your bones."

This was gold. I carefully wrote the quote on my notepad.

Porter followed that with a, "Don't print that ... until after we win it." He didn't want to provide any bulletin-board material. But really, his statement had nothing

LEFT: Merritt Paulson hoists the MLS Cup after the Timbers won the MLS Cup final. Randy L. Rasmussen/The Oregonian/OregonLive

OPPOSITE: Liam Ridgewell and his teammates greet fans at Providence Park two days after winning the MLS Cup final. Diego Valeri's goal just 27 seconds into the final match not only set a record for fastest goal in an MLS final, it epitomized the juggernaut the Timbers had become. Thomas Boyd/The Oregonian/OregonLive

to do with the opposition. Porter knew he had the best team at the right time and it didn't matter who showed up on game day – the Timbers were going to win.

The 5-year old expansion franchise with the ninth-highest payroll schooled the rest of the league. Also, they provided a decent blueprint for success. This franchise has become a thing of beauty.

The Timbers didn't get every decision correct. But what they did, whether it came to personnel or coaching, is course-correct quickly. They also were incredibly honest with themselves when they missed on a player or coach. They didn't follow mistakes with more mistakes. They didn't mistake hernias for hiccups. Paulson and his staff acted like an organization that understood how to get to the winner's circle.

It's why when Paulson announced last week that he'd be interested in buying the Trail Blazers someday that it was met with enthusiasm. The question, if you heard it, wasn't, "Does he know basketball?" Rather, it was, "Does he have the money?"

Henry Paulson, the Timbers majority owner and former Secretary of the Treasury, has a net worth estimated at somewhere between $700 million and $1 billion. So yeah. If Paul Allen wants to sell someday, an ownership group led by the Paulsons would be at the front of the line. And given the success they've fostered in MLS, they'd be welcomed with open arms by this market.

As the MLS playoffs began, Paulson texted me, "Need to win it this year."

You could sense the urgency and the congruency of vision in every corner of the organization. In fact, after

taking a 3-1 lead over Dallas in the opening leg of the Western Conference Final, Chief Operating Officer Mike Golub and team mascot "Timber Joey" Webber found themselves standing in front of Providence Park on the same curb, preparing to leave for home.

They nodded at each other like assembly line workers on the same mission. I figure when Diego Valeri scored the fastest goal in MLS Cup history (27 seconds into the match) he was just carrying out the finishing touches. The magnificence of the Timbers this season isn't that they were carried by a hired gun, but that every element of the organization felt galvanized.

Toward the end, it felt like Porter could have plucked some random member out of the Timbers Army on game day, coached the soul up, and won.

That's what is most impressive about what Paulson and the Timbers have accomplished. Fans bellyached at general manager Gavin Wilkinson over the years, sure.

But from ownership to the front office to the coaching staff to the players and beyond, this was a machine that rarely felt as if it got in its own way. Too many sports organizations wobble so badly internally they can't begin to move forward.

To the Timbers fans who were there all along, the rest of us envy you. It's been more journey than ride for some. But a fascinating thing happened somewhere along the way – maybe on that wild Thursday night when that soccer ball went post to post. People who never much cared about soccer suddenly became interested in this team.

"The more, the merrier," Paulson said.

On Sunday, with the championship winding down and the Timbers holding that one-goal advantage, people scrambled to share the updates. Citizens who have never seen a Timbers game, asked me if I knew the best way to track an MLS game on a smart phone.

An NFL or NBA game, they knew. What they were really saying was, "Man, a team that belongs to this city winning? What a blast!"

I wonder if Porter, who now has an NCAA title and an MLS title, will get a shot someday at coaching the U.S. Men's National team. He's hinted at wanting redemption there as Porter coached a U.S. Men's Olympic-qualifying team (U-23) that lost to Canada and failed to qualify for the London Olympics.

Porter calls it, "My career low point."

I wonder, too, if the Timbers roster of players will get picked over by international poachers. For example, how much longer will Darlington Nagbe belong to Portland? Also, I don't know if the enthusiasm generated by the purest soccer team in America will result in more enthusiastic interest in the sport.

Those questions are fair, but also feel far away.

A friend asked after hearing Portland won a championship, "Are we supposed to turn over a car or something?"

Not how this city rolls.

At least I hope not.

In the summer of 1977, Portland held a parade for the Trail Blazers. People climbed lampposts to get a better view. The photographs from that scene are burned in my mind. And so the question left about the Timbers is a simple one – when does the parade start? ■

ABOVE LEFT: Whether they've been supporting the team for 40 years or a few weeks, fans came out to show their support of the Timbers as they paraded through downtown Portland two days after winning the MLS Cup final. Randy L. Rasmussen/The Oregonian/OregonLive

LEFT: Darlington Nagbe and Caleb Porter celebrate with fans at Providence Park after winning the MLS Cup final. Porter and Nagbe now have an MLS title to go along with the NCAA title from 2010, which they won when Porter was coaching Nagbe with the Akron Zips. Thomas Boyd/The Oregonian/OregonLive

CONTENDERS

Making of an iconic front page

The Oregonian/OregonLive
DEC. 8, 2015

In the chaotic melee after the Timbers won the MLS Cup in Columbus, The Oregonian/OregonLive photographer Randy Rasmussen crouched on the field just as the players passed the cup around – each hoisting it above their head.

Rasmussen's photograph of Nat Borchers would become an instant classic. But it almost didn't make the cover.

Rasmussen and fellow The Oregonian/OregonLive photographer Thomas Boyd transmitted a flurry of photographs back to Portland following the conclusion of the Timbers' historic victory. Back in our newsroom, front page designer Fran Genovese combed through the options.

Genovese began to pull some of the more promising photos onto pages. "I had an idea of how I wanted the cover to look typographically," she said. "But until I married the words with the photos, I wasn't sure how it would work."

Genovese played around with several versions, including ones with Liam Ridgewell, Darlington Nagbe and Borchers holding the trophy. The photos were strong. But it's a team win and a team sport. Genovese was hoping for a group shot that would capture the Timbers reveling in the moment.

Design Leader Jody Stott, designer Shawn Barkdull and Sports curator Breen Newcomer huddled to review options, including a sideways design. The sideways option was immediately tossed out.

Genovese and the group initially settled on the team shot for the cover and it was sent to a small group of senior newsroom editors who always get a sneak peek at the front page before it goes to the pressroom. "I thought it was OK, she said. "But I wasn't in love with it. Breen took another look at the Borchers cover version and said he loved that one. So Jody asked me to finalize that one and send it out to the group."

The alternate cover got a strong reaction from Editor Mark Katches. He felt the team shot was a little cliché and flat. "The Borchers photo, on the other hand, was arresting and unique. You just don't see that photo every day. Still, I was a little worried that it was a photo of one individual when the victory was so much more than about one guy."

Katches and Stott jumped on the phone and they debated the merits of the covers. "The Borchers photo is the bolder choice," said Stott as she made her case.

"Let's be bold," Katches said. ∎

FINAL SELECTION

Cup Comes Home: Thousands descend on Providence Park to celebrate

By Jamie Goldberg

DEC. 8, 2015

The celebration was supposed to last only half an hour. But more than an hour after the program began, the Portland Timbers remained on the stage at Providence Park leading the crowd of more than 9,000 fans in off-key renditions of "Don't Stop Believin'" and "We Are the Champions."

After a memorable downtown parade, the Timbers capped off their MLS Cup championship celebration with a rally at Providence Park on Dec. 8.

The rain pounded down on the stadium and the wind blew so fiercely that it knocked a gigantic "Rose City" sign off the stage. But the weather didn't deter either the fans or the players.

As the players made their way onto the stage, the crowd broke into a rumbling cheer of "hey, Portland Timbers, we salute you." The song only grew louder as Liam Ridgewell carried the MLS Cup onto the stage.

The ceremony began with Portland Mayor Charlie Hales leading the crowd in a cheer of "when I root, I root for the Timbers" and Timbers owner Merritt Paulson jubilantly thanking the fans, before screaming, "This is Soccer City, USA" into the microphone.

After half a dozen Timbers players stepped to the microphone and thanked the supporters, Timbers coach Caleb Porter finally walked to the front of the stage.

"To win an MLS Cup, it takes an army," Porter said.

"You are that army."

Porter then led his players onto the Timbers Army capo stand at the north end of Providence Park. They stood below the sea of fans and held up the shining MLS Cup trophy as the crowd cheered.

"My favorite chant that you guys do is the 'we salute you,'" Porter said. "I hear you guys salute me and the players all the time and, so, this time we salute you."

The Timbers Army once again broke out into a heartfelt chant of "hey, Portland Timbers, we salute you" as the players sang along and danced with the trophy.

The Timbers closed out the official portion of the ceremony with the celebratory sawing of log slabs for the two goals scored by the Timbers in the MLS Cup. Timber Joey cut the first log slab for Diego Valeri's opening goal and invited Timber Jim, the club's original mascot on stage, to saw off the second slab for Rodney Wallace's game-winning goal.

Valeri and Wallace raised their log slabs in the air as the rest of their teammates gathered around them. Fireworks shot into the sky and the crowd continued to sing.

But when the fireworks stopped and Timbers broadcaster Jake Zivin attempted to bring the celebration to a close, the players stopped him.

They wanted to keep celebrating with their fans. ■

ABOVE: Retired Portland Timbers mascot Timber Jim hoists a Timbers Army scarf during a MLS Cup victory rally held at Providence Park on Dec. 8. Thomas Boyd/The Oregonian/OregonLive

OPPOSITE: Diego Valeri (left) and Rodney Wallace present slabs sliced from the victory log that they earned for scoring goals during the Portland Timbers' win in the MLS Cup final at a fan rally held at Providence Park on Dec. 8. Thomas Boyd/The Oregonian/OregonLive

ABOVE: Forward Fanendo Adi (right) presents the MLS Cup to a throng of fans who turned up at Portland International Airport and welcomed the Portland Timbers following their return home from Columbus, Ohio. Stephanie Yao Long/The Oregonian/OregonLive

OPPOSITE: Coach Caleb Porter (right) greets a fan as the MLS Cup Champion Portland Timbers parade through the streets of downtown Portland on Dec. 8. Randy L. Rasmussen/The Oregonian/OregonLive

ABOVE: Coach Caleb Porter is swarmed by fans as he carries the MLS Cup toward the crowd at Portland International Airport after capturing the trophy in Columbus, Ohio, the previous day.

Stephanie Yao Long/The Oregonian/OregonLive

LEFT: Portland Timbers players snap photos and enjoy their moment of celebration during an MLS Cup victory parade on the streets of downtown Portland on Dec. 8.

Randy L. Rasmussen/The Oregonian/OregonLive

OPPOSITE: Nat Borchers hoists the MLS Cup and carries it toward the raucous crowd that came out to Portland International Airport and welcomed the team home on Dec. 7.

Stephanie Yao Long/The Oregonian/OregonLive

ABOVE: Defender Alvas Powell (center) poses for a photo between two young fans during an MLS Cup victory parade on the streets of downtown Portland on Dec. 8. Randy L. Rasmussen/The Oregonian/OregonLive

ABOVE RIGHT: A Timbers fan raises a scarf above his head to acknowledge the players passing by during an MLS Cup victory parade on the streets of downtown Portland on Dec. 8.
Randy L. Rasmussen/The Oregonian/OregonLive

RIGHT: Owner Merritt Paulson and the MLS Champion Portland Timbers parade through downtown Portland on Dec. 8.
Randy L. Rasmussen/The Oregonian/OregonLive

OPPOSITE: Green lights illuminate the cold and heavy rain that fell during a victory rally for fans and Portland Timbers players held at Providence Park on Dec. 8, after the team returned home with the MLS Cup. Stephanie Yao Long/The Oregonian/OregonLive

ABOVE, LEFT AND OPPOSITE: Despite cold and heavy rain, Timbers fans arrived in numbers to sing, cheer and celebrate with the team during a victory rally held at Providence Park on Dec. 8 after the team returned home with the MLS Cup. Thomas Boyd/The Oregonian/OregonLive

ABOVE LEFT: Midfielder George Fochive (right) leads Portland Timbers players in a chant that he picked up during his childhood playing with youth soccer teams during a rally held at Providence Park on Dec. 8. Thomas Boyd/The Oregonian/OregonLive

ACKNOWLEDGMENTS

Story Editors: Ben Sherman and Tim Brown

Photo Editor: Mike Zacchino

Copy Editor: Nora Simon

Reporters: Jamie Goldberg, Molly Blue, John Canzano

Photographers: Thomas Boyd, Randy L. Rasmussen, Stephanie Yao Long, Beth Nakamura, Kristyna Wentz-Graff, Stewart F. House

Editor and Vice President of Content: Mark Katches

Special Thanks: Chris Hammond, Therese Bottomly, Hallie Janssen, Max Radi, Joel Odom, Karly Imus, Dennis Peck, Michelle Nicolosi, Jody Stott, Paul Gelormino, Mike Swanson

Amazing city...
World-class soccer...
One proud sponsor!

Sunset Porsche and Audi Beaverton, inaugural luxury vehicle sponsors of the Portland Timbers, have been proud to be a part of such an amazing franchise. We congratulate the Timbers on their 2015 MLS Cup win, and look forward cheering our team on for years to come. #RCTID

SUNSET PORSCHE

Audi Beaverton

Congrats to the Portland Timbers!

From all of KeyBank, congratulations to the
Portland Timbers, 2015 MLS Champions!

KeyBank ✚⚷®

Exclusive Retail and Commercial Bank of the Timbers.

Congratulations MLS Champions!